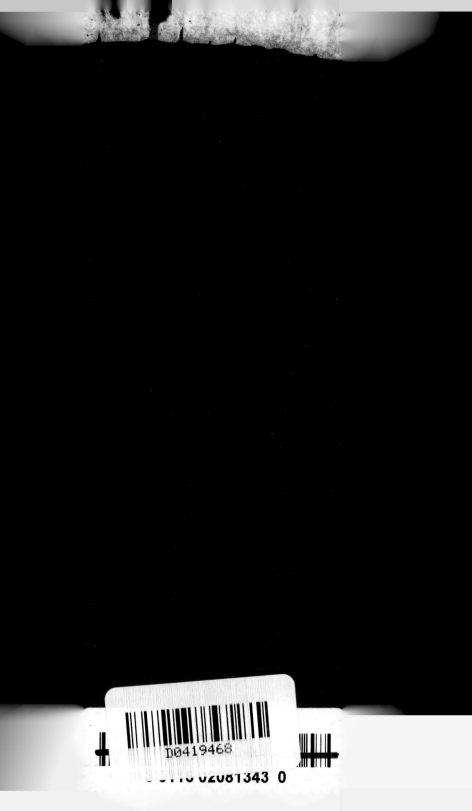

BOHEMIAN LONDON

BOHEMIAN LONDON

From Pre-Raphaelites to Punk

NICK RENNISON

Oldcastle Books

First published in 2017 by
Oldcastle Books Ltd,
PO Box 394, Harpenden,
Herts, AL5 1XJ
noexit.co.uk

A CIP catalogue record for this book is available from the British Library.

ISBN
978-1-904048-30-5 (print)
978-1-84344-819-8 (epub)
978-1-84344-820-4 (kindle)
978-1-84344-821-1 (pdf)

2 4 6 8 10 9 7 5 3 1

Typeset in 10.5pt Goudy Oldstyle
by Elsa Mathern
Printed and bound by Clays Ltd, St Ives Plc

Contents

BOHEMIAN LONDON

Introduction

'"Bohemia"... is both a state of mind and a place'
ROBERT HEWISON, *Under Siege*

LONDON has always been home to outsiders. To people who won't, or can't, abide by the conventions of respectable society. For close to two centuries these misfit individualists have had a name. They have been called bohemians. This book aims to provide a short introduction to bohemian London. It opens with a chapter devoted to those writers and artists, from the Renaissance to the Romantic era, who were bohemians before the word, in its current sense, was invented. It moves on to the creation of modern 'bohemia' in 1830s and 1840s Paris and to its incarnation across the Channel a few years later. The chapters that follow explore the world of London bohemians across a dozen decades. Rossetti and Swinburne, defying the morality of High Victorian England. Oscar Wilde and Aubrey Beardsley in the decadent 1890s. The Bloomsburyites and the Bright Young Things. Dylan Thomas, boozing in the Blitz, and Francis Bacon and his cronies, wasting time and getting wasted in 1950s Soho. It concludes with the punks of the 1970s and a chapter that looks at what has happened to London's bohemia in the last forty years.

This is a story of places as well as people, a matter of topography as well as biography. The history of bohemian London can be traced across a map of the capital from Chelsea and Bloomsbury to Soho and Fitzrovia. And just as no such history should omit, say, Francis Bacon or Nina Hamnett, no record of it can ignore the pubs and clubs in which they and their fellows drank, talked and swapped ideas. The legendary Café Royal, a home from home to artists and writers for nearly a century. The Cave of the Golden Calf, a First World War nightclub run by the Swedish playwright August Strindberg's widow. The Colony Room, the infamous drinking den presided over by the gloriously foul-mouthed Muriel Belcher, and the Gargoyle Club in Dean Street where the artistic avant-garde mixed with upper-crust eccentrics. The Fitzroy Tavern and the Wheatsheaf where the painter Augustus John rubbed shoulders with the occultist Aleister Crowley, and the short-story writer Julian Maclaren-Ross, wearing mirror sunglasses and clutching a silver-topped Malacca cane, held court for his acolytes and admirers.

The history of bohemian London is one of drink and drugs, sex and death, excess and indulgence. It's also one of achievement and success. Some of the finest art and literature of the last two centuries has emerged from bohemia. It is a complicated history which a book of this length can only outline in its essentials, but it is also, as I hope I have made clear in the following pages, endlessly fascinating.

Chapter One

BOHEMIA BEFORE IT HAD A NAME

Shakespearean Rogues and Restoration Roisterers

TO SHAKESPEARE and his contemporaries, the word 'Bohemia' would have signified nothing more than the name of a faraway country of which they knew little. In *The Winter's Tale*, the Bard famously gets his geography in a muddle and gives Bohemia a coast on the sea when it had none. During the Elizabethan and Jacobean eras, the use of 'bohemian' to describe the unconventional or the artistic was 250 years in the future. Yet many of the playwrights of Shakespeare's day lived lives that would have undoubtedly been labelled 'bohemian' in later centuries. Indeed, some were far more extreme in their flouting of ordinary morality than their descendants in the nineteenth and twentieth centuries. Later bohemians mostly contented themselves with sex, drugs, drink and not paying their bills. More than one Elizabethan dramatist committed murder. John Day, who had already been expelled from Caius College, Cambridge for stealing books, stabbed to death his fellow playwright Henry Porter in a quarrel in Southwark in 1599. He pleaded guilty to manslaughter, but seems later to have gained a Royal Pardon for his offence. Ben Jonson, author of *Volpone* and *The Alchemist*, who once described Day as a 'rogue' and 'base fellow', had himself killed a man the previous year. During a duel in Hoxton, Jonson ended the life of an actor named Gabriel Spenser. He spent time in jail, but was able to escape worse punishment by pleading 'benefit of clergy', taking advantage of an old law which excluded the clergy (or, in Jonson's case, a literate man who could prove his knowledge of Latin) from condemnation by a secular court. He emerged from Newgate Prison with no more than a branded thumb. The most famous of all Shakespeare's contemporaries, Christopher Marlowe, led a notably rackety life. Accused in his lifetime of atheism, he was also reported to have said that 'all they who love not tobacco and boys are fools'. He met his end in May 1593 in a Deptford drinking den. Stabbed in the head during what was said to be a brawl over payment of the bill, the greatest dramatist before the advent of Shakespeare may have been a victim of the shady world of espionage in which he sometimes operated.

Although he died at the age of only 29 and his fame was rapidly eclipsed by that of Shakespeare, Marlowe's gifts were not forgotten and his plays have continued to be regularly performed. The same cannot be said of the man who, more than any other writer of the day, embodied the characteristics we would now call 'bohemian'. Today, Robert Greene is primarily remembered, if he is remembered at all, for a single disparaging comment about Shakespeare that he made in a pamphlet. *Greene's Groatsworth of Wit, Bought with a Million of Repentance* includes a description of an unnamed dramatist, assumed to be Shakespeare, as an 'upstart crow'. It was published in the September of 1592, two weeks after its author had died, allegedly of a surfeit of pickled herring and Rhenish wine, at the age of 34. (Scholarly debate still continues over the question

UNKNOWN 21-YEAR OLD MAN, SUPPOSED TO BE CHRISTOPHER MARLOWE, 1585, ARTIST UNKNOWN

of whether Greene wrote the words for which he is most famous or they were put posthumously into his pamphlet by someone else, probably fellow writer Henry Chettle.) During his lifetime, Greene was renowned both for his writing and his dissolute way of life. A graduate of Cambridge, he nonetheless revelled in the low life of London, spending much of his time in the city's least reputable taverns and taking as his mistress the sister of a notorious criminal known as 'Cutting Ball' who was hanged at Tyburn.

The years of the Civil War and Oliver Cromwell's rule were not ones likely to encourage bohemianism, although they did see the emergence of several groups who advocated what might today be called 'alternative lifestyles'. The Diggers, for example, under the leadership of Gerrard Winstanley, established what was, in effect, a commune on land at St George's Hill, Surrey until the violent opposition of local landlords forced them to abandon it. When the monarchy was restored under Charles II, free rein was given to the kind of aristocratic bad behaviour which can be retrospectively labelled 'bohemian'. The court was filled with upper-class reprobates such as those Samuel Pepys met on 30 May 1668 when he 'fell into the company of Harry Killigrew... and young Newport and others, as very rogues as any in the town who were ready to take hold of every woman who come by them'. According to Pepys, 'their mad bawdy talk did make my heart ache', but there is no mistaking the prurient delight with which the diarist reported how his new chums told him of a 'meeting of some young blades... and my Lady Bennet and her ladies and their there dancing naked, and all the roguish things of the world'. 'Lord, what loose cursed company was this that I was in tonight,' Pepys concludes, although admitting that it was 'full of wit; and worth a man's being in for once, to know the nature of it, and their manner of talk, and lives.'

One of Charles II's favourites was the dissolute poet and courtier, John Wilmot, 2nd Earl of Rochester, who, in the resounding words of Dr Johnson, 'blazed out his youth and health in lavish voluptuousness'. What Johnson actually meant was that Rochester, like so many bohemians to come, devoted enormous amounts of his time and energy to sex and drink. A poem of the era, written either by or about him, gives a picture of his dissipations which is graphic even by modern standards. The poet describes his typical day: 'I rise at eleven, I dine about two/I get drunk before seven, and the next thing I do/I send for my whore, when for fear of a clap/I spend in her hand and I spew in her lap.' The day goes from bad to worse as, unsurprisingly, the woman decides she has had

PORTRAIT OF JOHN WILMOT, 2ND EARL OF ROCHESTER
BY JACOB HUYSMANS, 1665-1670

enough of her ungallant lover and disappears with the contents of his purse. 'I storm and I roar, and I fall in a rage/And missing my whore, I bugger my page/Then, crop-sick all morning, I rail at my men/And in bed I lie yawning till eleven again.' When not bedding whores and pages or boozing the day away, Rochester was indulging in vendettas and dubiously ethical pranks. He is alleged to have arranged for thugs to beat up rival poet John Dryden, whom he wrongly suspected of writing an anonymous satire in which he was lampooned. (The attack took place near the Lamb and Flag pub in Rose Street, Covent Garden and the site is still marked by a plaque.) On several occasions he adopted the persona of a charlatan healer named Dr Bendo, with premises near Tower

Hill, whose specialisation in gynaecological health gave him privileged access to married women. Worn out by his indulgences, and suffering from the combined effects of syphilis, gonorrhoea and alcoholism, Rochester died in 1680 at the age of 33.

Among Rochester's fellow poets and companions in aristocratic hell-raising were Charles Sackville, 6th Earl of Dorset, and Sir Charles Sedley, who outraged public opinion in June 1663 by getting appallingly drunk at a pub in Bow Street called, appropriately enough in view of what happened, the Cock Tavern. According to Samuel Johnson, in his eighteenth-century life of Dorset, the two men went on to the pub's balcony and 'exposed themselves to the populace in very indecent postures'. As people booed and bayed for their blood in the street below, Sedley stripped himself entirely naked and harangued the crowd 'in such profane language that the public indignation was awakened'. Amidst riotous scenes, the drunken poets were driven from the balcony by a shower of stones and later had to face the wrath of the magistrates, who fined Sedley the then huge sum of £500.

Grub Street

In the eighteenth century poverty-stricken poets and writers were not called 'bohemians'; they were denizens of 'Grub Street'. Grub Street was a street in Moorfields, which, in the late seventeenth and early eighteenth centuries, was, in the words of Samuel Johnson, 'much inhabited by writers of small histories, dictionaries and temporary poems'. Renamed Milton Street in the nineteenth century, it has now been swallowed up by the Barbican development. In Johnson's day, Grub Street had not only a topographical reality, but a metaphorical meaning. It became the term applied generally to hack writers and their work, to those who scrabbled and scribbled to make a living in the margins of the literary world. Most of what they churned out was terrible dross, although representative Grub Street figures like the proto-journalist and satirist Tom Brown (1662–1704) and the publican-turned-versifier Ned Ward (1667–1731) sometimes chronicled the urban spectacle of early eighteenth-century London with energy and vigour. Brown's *Amusements Serious and Comical, Calculated for the Meridian of London* presents the city as seen through the eyes of both the narrator and an imaginary visitor from India. Ward's *The London Spy* offers an entertaining panorama of contemporary London life from coffee-house wits to Billingsgate fishwives, from the inhabitants of Bedlam to the courtiers at St James's Palace.

The greatest contemporary portrait of Grub Street comes in *The Dunciad*, Alexander Pope's scathing denunciation of a literary world presided over by the goddess Dullness, first published in 1728 and revised over the next 15 years. In blisteringly witty verse, Pope holds up a succession of hacks and poetasters for ridicule. It's the same world conjured up by William Hogarth's image of *The Distrest Poet*, which he produced first as an oil painting in 1736 and published as an engraving a few years later. Indeed, the artist may well have been inspired by a reading of *The Dunciad*. In a garret room, the harassed versifier struggles to put pen to paper, distracted by the presence of his wife, a crying baby and a milkmaid just arrived at the door to demand payment of her bill. Like Pope, Hogarth has a moral purpose in depicting the scene as he does, but there is no reason to believe that *The Distrest Poet* does not reflect something of the reality of Grub Street in its heyday.

Nearly all those unfortunates lambasted by Pope have long been forgotten, their only memorials the lines with which he excoriated them. However, two distinguished literary figures, at least, did emerge from Grub Street. One was Oliver Goldsmith. Later famous as the author of the novel *The Vicar of Wakefield* and the play *She Stoops to Conquer*, the Irishman produced tens of thousands of words for very little money during his early days in London. On several occasions he was reduced to staying within the

DR SAMUEL JOHNSON READING THE MANUSCRIPT OF OLIVER GOLDSMITH'S
'THE VICAR OF WAKEFIELD', WHILST A BAILIFF WAITS WITH THE LANDLADY.
MEZZOTINT BY S. BELLIN, 1845, AFTER E.M. WARD

confines of his grubby garret room where the only furniture was a
single wooden chair and a window-bench because, in the words of
an early biographer, 'his clothes had become too ragged to submit
to daylight scrutiny'. Samuel Johnson tells the story of receiving
a frantic message from Goldsmith whose landlady had had him
arrested for non-payment of rent. Johnson took possession of the
manuscript of *The Vicar of Wakefield* and sold it to a publisher for
£60 which rescued Goldsmith from his debt.

Johnson was himself the other great survivor of Grub Street
in eighteenth-century literature. He arrived in London from his
native Lichfield in 1737. He is now remembered as the imposing
figure created by Boswell in his biography, but, before he established
his name with the publication of his monumental *Dictionary of the
English Language* in 1755, he was obliged to churn out vast reams of

poems, essays and journalism, all of it for very little money. One of these Grub Street works, first published anonymously in 1744, was his *Life of Richard Savage*. If Johnson was a Grub Street escapee, able through luck and his own talents and endeavours to move beyond it, Richard Savage was a man who (metaphorically) lived his entire life there. Johnson knew him and, indeed, developed a close friendship with the older man soon after he came to London. The two spent entire nights pacing the city, engaged in lengthy discussions of poetry and politics. Savage was probably born in London and probably in 1697, although the circumstances of his birth are as disputed as many of the rest of the details of his ramshackle life. (In later years, he became obsessively convinced that he was the bastard son of the Countess of Macclesfield, abandoned soon after his birth, and he pursued his alleged mother relentlessly in person and in print.) As a young man, he earned a precarious living by writing poetry and plays, some of which were staged at the Theatre Royal, Drury Lane. In 1727, Savage, always quarrelsome and short-tempered, became embroiled in a sword fight in a Charing Cross brothel and killed a man. Convicted of murder, but pardoned through the intercession of an aristocratic admirer, he entered a period of comparative fame and wealth, lauded for a long poem entitled *The Wanderer*, but soon managed to sabotage his own good fortune and re-enter a world of poverty and exile from decent society.

Johnson's words about his ill-fated friend could well be applied to thousands of bohemian souls as yet unborn when Savage died in 1743, a penniless debtor, in a prison in Bristol. The poet was a *bon vivant* who was never 'the first of the company that desired to separate'. He was always short of cash and yet always prepared to spend other people's. 'It was the constant practice of Mr Savage to enter a tavern with any company that proposed it,' Johnson wrote, 'drink the most expensive wines with great profusion, and when the reckoning was demanded, to be without money.' Like

RICHARD SAVAGE : A ROMANCE OF REAL LIFE, CHARLES WHITEHEAD, 1844

all bohemians past and present, he was an enemy of domesticity. 'Being always accustomed to an irregular manner of life,' his friend Johnson concluded, 'he could not confine himself to any stated hours, or pay any regard to the rules of a family, but would prolong his conversation to midnight, without considering that business might require his friend's application in the morning; and, when he had persuaded himself to retire to bed, was not, without equal difficulty, called up to dinner; it was therefore impossible to pay him any distinction without the entire subversion of all economy, a kind of establishment which, wherever he went, he always appeared ambitious to overthrow.'

One of the areas through which Johnson and Savage regularly walked during their nocturnal perambulations was Covent Garden, which has some claims to being London's first bohemian quarter. In the eighteenth century, it was a place of sexual freedom where prostitution flourished. *Harris's List of Covent Garden Ladies*, first published in 1757 and updated annually for some years thereafter, listed the names, addresses, physical charms and sexual specialities of more than 100 women who worked as prostitutes in the area. 'This accomplished nymph has just attained her eighteenth year,' runs one typical entry, 'and fraught with every perfection, enters a volunteer in the field of Venus. She plays on the pianoforte, sings, dances, and is mistress of every maneuver in the amorous contest that can enhance the coming pleasure.' The poetically elevated language cannot ultimately disguise the basic financial transaction that is being advertised. The accomplished nymph's entry in the list ends: 'Her price, two pounds.' Although it was published under the name of Jack Harris, a well-known pimp of the day, *Harris's List* was almost certainly compiled by an archetypal inhabitant of Grub Street named Samuel Derrick. Derrick reputedly produced the first edition of the book and sold it to a publisher as a means of getting the money to release himself from debtors' prison. For some time he was the lover of a well-known actress named Jane Lessingham and was considered something of a womaniser, although, as one unfriendly journalist wrote, 'he was of a diminutive size, with reddish hair and a vacant countenance; and he required no small quantity of perfume to predominate over some odours that were not of the most fragrant kind.'

Covent Garden was also home to many of the era's molly houses, meeting places for gay men. These were intended to be safe spaces in which they could dress and behave as they wished. A witness to a costume ball in one of the molly houses reported that, 'The men were calling one another "my dear" and hugging, kissing and tickling each other as if they were a mixture of wanton males and females, and assuming effeminate voices and airs… Some were completely rigged in gowns, petticoats, headcloths, fine laced shoes, furbelowed scarves, and masks; some had riding hoods; some were dressed like milkmaids, others like shepherdesses…' Of course, they were not always safe. The most notorious of the molly houses (which was actually in Holborn rather than Covent Garden) was Mother Clap's and it gained its fame because of a raid on its premises in 1726. Forty men were arrested and, in a series of trials at the Old Bailey which followed, the 'alternative lifestyle' pursued by the 'mollies' was revealed. One witness, who had gone undercover at Mother Clap's, described what he had seen: 'I found near fifty men there, making love to one another as they called it. Sometimes they'd sit in one another's laps, use their hands indecently, dance and make curtsies and mimic the Language of Women – "O Sir! - Pray Sir! - Dear Sir! Lord how can ye serve me so! - Ah ye little dear Toad!" Then they'd go by couples, into a room on the same floor to be married as they called it.' It all sounds perfectly harmless, but the consequences, for some unlucky men, were terrible. As a result of the raid on Mother Clap's and the series of trials that followed, at least three were hanged and others endured the ordeal of standing in the pillory.

Like Soho in years to come, Covent Garden in the eighteenth century was not just the prime London venue for illicit sex. The area also attracted artists and writers. Some, like JMW Turner, who was born in Maiden Lane, the son of a hairdresser, and continued to lodge in the neighbourhood during his early success as a painter, were famous; others were more obscure. Many of them were ferocious drinkers. Francis Hayman, who began his career as a scene painter in the Theatre Royal, Drury Lane and became a founding member of the Royal Academy in 1768, was a regular six-bottles-a-day man.

One night, crossing Covent Garden Piazza with his friend, the actor James Quin, both men were so drunk that, when they fell into the gutter, they were unable to get out of it and had to wait for the night watchmen to haul them out. Figure and landscape painter John Hamilton Mortimer, another Covent Garden regular, made the mistake of eating a wine glass during one of his many drinking bouts – 'of which act of folly he never recovered', according to a contemporary. He died at the age of only 39 in 1779.

Nearby Soho also had its drunken and impoverished artists in these years. Samuel Collings, a caricaturist who was a friend of Thomas Rowlandson, died on the steps of a tavern while in his cups. A *trompe l'oeil* painter named Capitsoldi, probably an Italian who had moved to the city, was so penniless he couldn't afford to furnish his lodgings in Warwick Street. Ingeniously, he 'proceeded to paint chairs, pictures and window curtains on the walls of his sitting room… so admirably executed that, with an actual table and a couple of real chairs, he was able to entertain on occasion a friend in an apartment that appeared adequately furnished'. Some artists of the day suffered even worse fates than near destitution. The Swiss-born Théodore Gardelle murdered his landlady, a Mrs Anna King, in Leicester Square in 1761. He left her body lying in the house for several days, telling visitors that she was away in the West Country, but eventually had to undertake what the *Newgate Calendar* called 'the horrid employment of cutting the body to pieces, and disposing of it in different places'. It was not an easy job. 'The bowels he threw down the necessary,' the anonymous author in the *Calendar* continued, 'and the flesh of the body and limbs cut to pieces, he scattered about the cock-loft, where he supposed they would dry and perish without putrefaction'. He was wrong and his crime was eventually discovered more than a week after poor Mrs King had died. Gardelle was tried at the Old Bailey, found guilty and hanged in the Haymarket.

Romantics and Rebels

Nearly a decade after Richard Savage died in Bristol, another forerunner of English bohemianism was born in the same city. Thomas Chatterton was the son of a schoolmaster and musician who had died some months before the future poet arrived in the world on 20 November 1752. He and his mother and sister lived in genteel poverty near the medieval church of St Mary Redcliffe which became Chatterton's favourite haunt as he grew up. Obsessed by the Middle Ages – or, at least, the version of them he created in his imagination – he began writing verse when still a child. He moved to London in 1770, already the author of a series of pseudo-archaic poems he had attributed to an imaginary, fifteenth-century monk named Thomas Rowley. His intention was to earn a living with his pen, but his poems and articles for the capital's press did not bring in enough money to support him. He continued to write, but he was soon starving and desperate. In August 1770, after only a few months in London and still not 18 years old, he committed suicide by taking arsenic in the attic room he rented in Brooke Street, Holborn.

Chatterton made little impact on his contemporaries, but his short life and despairing death at his own hand had a powerful effect on generations to come. 'The marvellous boy', as Wordsworth called him, became an iconic figure in the Romantic imagination. Throughout the nineteenth century, perhaps most famously in the painting *The Death of Chatterton* by Henry Wallis (now in Tate Britain), he was depicted as the epitome of doomed bohemianism, a youthful genius fated to die in a garret, his brilliant talents unrecognised. (The model for Chatterton in Wallis's painting was the poet and novelist George Meredith. Wallis later repaid Meredith by running off with his wife, providing the writer with material for his 1859 novel *The Ordeal of Richard Feverel*, considered unspeakably shocking in its sexual frankness by its mid-

THE DEATH OF CHATTERTON, HENRY WALLIS, 1856

Victorian audience. 'I am tabooed from all decent drawing-room tables,' Meredith wrote.) There was something about Chatterton's death that was both appalling and inspiring to those aspiring to literary greatness. The attraction was not restricted to Britain. The novelist, poet and dramatist, Alfred de Vigny, a major figure in the French Romantic Movement, wrote a play about Chatterton which was very successful in the 1830s and formed the basis for a later opera by the Italian composer Ruggero Leoncavallo.

The first generation of English Romantics, admirers all of 'the marvellous boy', flirted with bohemianism themselves in their youth. Robert Southey and William Wordsworth, both of whom became Poet Laureate, exuded conservatism and respectability in later life, but were more adventurous as young men. Southey dreamed of utopia and planned, with Samuel Taylor Coleridge, to establish an egalitarian community on the banks of the Susquehanna River in Pennsylvania. The dream soon foundered on the rocks of everyday practicalities and Southey's growing realisation that he wouldn't be able to employ servants to do the dirty work once he was in the New World. After a reduced plan to run a communal farm in Wales also came to nothing, Pantisocracy (as the two poets dubbed their political ideas) was abandoned. Wordsworth initially hailed the French Revolution ('Bliss was it in that dawn to be alive/But to be young was very heaven,' he later remembered), lived in France for some time and fathered a child with his French lover Annette Vallon. Southey's fellow Pantisocrat Coleridge was later plunged into dissipation and despair by his addiction to opium.

The next generation of English Romantic poets proved even more controversial than their predecessors. The deadening hand of mid-Victorian respectability was several decades in the future and Regency London was relatively forgiving of lapses in personal morality, but Shelley and Byron still managed to shock. Shelley was sent down from Oxford for arguing the benefits, indeed the necessity, of atheism and his love life soon scandalised his contemporaries. He eloped to Scotland with 16-year-old Harriet Westbrook, rescuing her from a girls' school in Clapham, where she was deeply unhappy, and heading north. The pair married and had a daughter, but their relationship was soon in trouble. Shelley met Mary Godwin, teenage daughter of the anarchist philosopher William Godwin and the pioneering feminist Mary Wollstonecraft, who had died giving birth to her. In 1814, after a series of clandestine rendezvous at Wollstonecraft's grave in St Pancras churchyard, they embarked on a love affair. Together with Mary's even younger stepsister Claire Clairmont, the couple fled to France. Disowned by both their families, they were forced by financial hardships to return to England, where Shelley often ignored the now pregnant Mary in favour of excursions with Claire. A noisy advocate of free love, the poet seemed eager to push his lover into the arms of his best friend Thomas Hogg, but Mary resisted the idea. Eventually, in 1816, the couple, still with Claire in tow, left for Lake Geneva and a summer in the company of Lord

Byron. That same year Harriet Shelley, miserable and possibly pregnant by another lover, drowned herself in the Serpentine.

Lord Byron, Shelley's and Mary's companion during that summer, was famously described by his former lover Lady Caroline Lamb as 'mad, bad and dangerous to know'. Rumoured to have had a sexual relationship with his half-sister Augusta Leigh, he had found himself *persona non grata* in England as a result and retired to the Continent where scandal still pursued him. Just before he left, he had had an affair with Claire Clairmont who gave birth to their daughter Allegra in January 1817. Byron wrote to a friend, 'I never loved her nor pretended to love her – but a man is a man – & if a girl of eighteen comes prancing to you at all hours of the night – there is but one way – the suite of all this is that she was with child – & returned to England to assist in peopling that desolate island.' Poor Allegra died at the age of five; her mother lived on until her eighties, regularly bemoaning the fact that her relationship with Byron had brought her a few moments of pleasure and a lifetime of trouble. Byron himself spent his last years in Italy, surrounded by mistresses and ladies of easy virtue, until he decided that his presence was required in Greece during the country's war of independence against the Ottoman Empire. He died of a fever at Missolonghi in western Greece in 1824.

In some ways the most bohemian of all the Romantics (if indeed he can be described as a Romantic) was the one who was the most remote and artistically isolated from his famous contemporaries. William Blake was a visionary whose verse won very little recognition in his own lifetime, but is now acknowledged as an extraordinary fusion of the material and the mundane with the spiritual and the transcendent. 'I must Create a System, or be enslav'd by another man's,' he once wrote and, in pursuit of his own particular interpretation of the world, he seemed odd, if not downright insane, to most of his contemporaries. (Wordsworth once remarked that, 'There was no doubt that this poor man was mad, but there is something in the madness of this man which interests me more than the sanity of Lord Byron and Walter Scott.') Blake had had visions since his childhood. At the age of four, he later reported, he had seen God outside his bedroom window and, five years later, he had been enthralled by 'a tree full of angels'. The visions continued into his adult life, shaping his view of the world and his art, but making Blake a difficult man with whom to have ordinary dealings. He was also markedly indifferent to everyday social conventions. A friend once found him and his wife sitting naked in their garden, reading *Paradise Lost*. When the friend hurriedly tried to retire, Blake is said to have called out, 'Come in, come in! It is only Adam and Eve, you know!' In his lifetime, Blake was known to very few outside a small circle of admirers. He died in poverty in rooms in Fountain Court off the Strand in 1827 and was buried in an unmarked grave in Bunhill Fields.

Blake's difficulties in making a living from his creative work are reminders that a version of Grub Street still survived in the first decades of the nineteenth century. An artist could find it as hard to thrive as a writer. (Being both, poor Blake had two vocations in which to fail to earn an adequate living.) Etched in 1812, Rowlandson's *Chamber of Genius* is a print which updates and echoes Hogarth's *Distrest Poet*, this time showing a painter struggling to create a masterpiece as domestic chaos reigns around him. Plenty of painters of the day could match Rowlandson's artist in the squalor of their circumstances. James Barry was an Irish artist whose grandiose series of paintings entitled *The Progress of Human Knowledge and Culture* can still be seen in the Great Room of the Royal Society of Arts in John Adam Street. He was also a man so paranoid and aggressive that he was the only Academician in the first 200 years of the Royal Academy's existence to be ejected from it, largely because of the insults he directed at his colleagues there. By the latter years of his life, he looked more like a tramp than an acclaimed artist. Just before he died in 1806, he was described by

WILLIAM BLAKE BY PHILLIPS SCHIAVONETTI

the poet Robert Southey as wearing 'an old coat of green baize…
from which time had taken all the green that incrustations of paint
and dirt had not covered. His wig was one which you might suppose
he had borrowed from a scarecrow; all round it there projected a
fringe of his own grey hair.' He lived alone in a house in a street off
Oxford Street 'which was never cleaned, and he slept on a bedstead
with no other furniture than a blanket nailed on the one side'.
Some locals believed he was a wizard who communicated with the
dead and took to throwing stones, bones and mud at the front of
the house to express their disapproval. Driven from the house by
their persecutions, he died of pleuritic fever in the home of one of
his few remaining friends, the architect Joseph Bonomi.

George Morland, born in Haymarket in 1763, came from a family of artists. Fuelled by drink and permanently in debt, Morland was obliged to churn out hundreds and hundreds of paintings in a desperate bid to stay one step ahead of his creditors. Obscene drawings and painted pub signs helped to pay for the beer he consumed in vast quantities. While on the run from those to whom he owed money, he visited the Isle of Wight. This was the time of the Napoleonic Wars and Morland's constant drawing and sketching of local landmarks was thought suspicious. He was arrested as a French spy and narrowly avoided imprisonment. Returning to London, he continued his career of drink and dodging creditors. He died in a sponging-house (a place where debtors were temporarily confined) in Coldbath Fields aged 41. His own suggestion for his epitaph was 'Here lies a drunken dog'.

Benjamin Haydon was 20 years younger than Morland. Friendly with many of the great names of the Romantic era, he was the host of a now famous dinner party in December 1817 at which John Keats was introduced to William Wordsworth and a very drunk Charles Lamb had to be locked in an adjoining room in order to prevent him from conducting an unwanted phrenological examination of another guest. A painter of limited genius but almost unlimited ambition, Haydon struggled all his life against poverty and what he saw as the poor taste of the art-buying public. He died in 1846. His work had long fallen out of what little favour it once possessed. The final indignity came when he exhibited his latest work at the Egyptian Hall in Piccadilly. The rival attraction was the American dwarf General Tom Thumb. Huge crowds flocked to see the minuscule General; hardly anyone looked at Haydon's paintings. 'Stretch me no longer on this rough world,' the artist wrote in a note and shot himself. Even in suicide he was not initially successful. The bullet failed to kill him and he had to resort to a cut-throat razor to finish himself off.

Chapter Two

NINETEENTH-CENTURY BOHEMIA

The Invention of Bohemia

BY THE TIME Benjamin Haydon met his sad end, bohemianism, as it was to be understood and imagined for the next 150 years and more, was already in the making across the Channel. In a sense, the idea of the bohemian that has become familiar today could not exist before the Romantics popularised a new image of the creative artist. In earlier centuries, as we have seen, there had certainly been writers and painters who lived disreputable and unruly lives, but it was the Romantic Movement that gave birth to the notion of the artist as outsider, a man (and it was nearly always a man) who rebelled against rules and conventions in order to pursue his own vision. A man who indulged to excess in drink, drugs and sex in search of experiences unknown to the ordinary, hidebound citizen. A man who scorned the traditional rewards and riches offered by society and was ready to embrace poverty if that was the only way he could remain true to himself and to his art. A bohemian, in other words.

It was in Paris that the new bohemian was born. The exact date of birth is difficult to pin down, but one important date during the pregnancy was 25 February 1830. This was the day on which Victor Hugo's play *Hernani* had its première. The first night became the battleground for the fight, metaphorically and at times literally, between the forces of the classical tradition in French theatre and the devotees of a new Romanticism focused on Hugo. The latter's supporters included the novelists Balzac and Dumas *père*, the flamboyant Théophile Gautier, who arrived dressed in 'a pair of pale sea-green trousers embellished at the seams with black velvet stripes, an ample grey coat faced in green satin, and a ribbon of mottled silk to perform the services more conventionally rendered by collar and tie', the composer Hector Berlioz, and the eccentric poet Gérard de Nerval, who regularly put his pet lobster on a leash and took it for a (presumably slow) walk through the Tuileries Gardens. This army of Romantics arrived in the theatre as an occupying force some hours before the curtain went up. Drinking the wine they had brought, they grew increasingly noisy as time passed and, when the play began, they indicated their approval with cheers and applause before the actors could get very far with Hugo's tangled tale of thwarted love in sixteenth-century Spain. Those in the audience who saw *Hernani* as the betrayal of all that was most precious in the French theatre responded with jeers and catcalls. The evening descended into chaos as different factions came to blows in the auditorium.

The earliest French bohemians emerged from the ranks of those who supported Hugo's play. In French, the word *bohémien* was used to refer to the Roma, the nomadic people known as 'gypsies' in English. Both words for the Roma are based on misunderstandings about their geographical origins. 'Gypsy' is a corruption of 'Egyptian', because they were thought to come from the Nile delta; *bohémien* indicates that the French believed the Roma had arrived in their country from Bohemia, the ancient

HENRI MURGER PHOTOGRAPHED BY NADAR, 1857

kingdom that is now part of the Czech Republic. In the 1820s and 1830s, *bohémien*, hitherto used exclusively to refer to the Roma, perennial outsiders in settled European societies, began to be used to describe those impoverished artists of the Romantic era who were supposed to lead similarly vagabond lives.

The man who gave greater currency to this new name for artistic exiles from bourgeois society was Henri Murger. Born in Paris in 1822, Murger left school at the age of 15 and worked for a time in a lawyer's office, but he yearned for success in the literary world. He published poetry, wrote journalism and essays for very little money, frequented the cafés and garrets of the Latin Quarter and joined a group of like-minded souls known as 'The Water Drinkers', because they were too poor to afford wine.

Beginning in 1845, he published in a small Parisian magazine a series of fictionalised sketches of the life he and his companions were leading. These tales of the poet Rodolphe, the artist Marcel, the philosopher Schaunard and their mistresses Mimi and Musette gained little attention until a successful playwright named Théodore Barrière approached Murger with the idea of dramatising them. (According to legend, the first meeting between the two men was hampered by Murger's unwillingness to get out of bed in his garret room. He had no trousers to wear to greet his visitor because he had just lent his only pair to a friend.) *La Vie de Bohème*, written by Murger and Barrière, had its première in November 1849 and became the theatrical sensation of the year. Two years later, the original sketches were collected in a volume entitled *Scènes de la vie bohème* and Murger's fortune looked to be made. It was not to be. Although he continued to publish novels throughout the 1850s, none of them had the same success as *La Vie de Bohème*. When he died in 1861, he was almost as penniless as he had been in his garret. His last words are reputed to have been, 'No noise, no music, no bohemia.'

'Bohemia is a stage in artistic life,' Murger wrote, 'it is the preface to the Academy, the Hôtel Dieu, or the Morgue.' In other words, bohemians were doomed to dull respectability, if they were lucky, and lifelong poverty or an early death, if they were not. His contemporary, the lawyer and writer Alphonse de Calonne, expressed it more bluntly. Bohemia, he wrote, was 'a sad country… bordered on the north by need, on the south by misery, on the east by illusion and on the west by the infirmary'.

Bohemia Arrives in London

Henri Murger was convinced that bohemia was a phenomenon peculiar to his own city. 'We will add that bohemia only exists and is only possible in Paris,' he wrote. He was wrong. An English equivalent had already sprung into life in London by the time he was writing. Throughout the nineteenth century, Paris was a destination for Englishmen in search of less respectable pleasures than those they felt able to seek in London. From Dickens and Wilkie Collins, touring the disreputable parts of the city on holiday jaunts, to Sir Arthur Sullivan, with his enthusiastic patronage of Parisian brothels, Victorian artists, writers and musicians found freedoms in the French capital that were unavailable in their own. It was inevitable that the Parisian idea of bohemianism would cross the Channel in some form or another.

One of the first to use the word 'bohemian' in English in its new, figurative sense was Thackeray, who had probably come across Murger's accounts of *la vie de bohème* when they were still no more than Parisian newspaper sketches. In *Vanity Fair*, first published in serial form in 1847 and 1848, he writes of his lively anti-heroine Becky Sharp that 'her taste for disrespectability grew more and more remarkable. She became a perfect Bohemian ere long, herding with people whom it would make your hair stand on end to meet.' Thackeray knew Paris well. He had studied art there as a young man and one of his first successes as a writer was with a travel book, *The Paris Sketch Book*. He must have encountered plenty of Rodolphes, Marcels and Schaunards in his time.

In fact, he also had exemplars of the bohemian life closer to hand. Thackeray was a friend to both William Maginn and Theodore Hook in the latter stages of their ramshackle careers. They appear, thinly disguised, as Captain Shandon and Mr Wagg in *Pendennis*, his autobiographical novel which first appeared in monthly instalments between 1848 and 1850. Both men led lives that, in their disorganisation and dissipation, were more than a match for those of any Parisian bohemians. Maginn, an Irishman from Cork, arrived in London in the 1820s, where he soon made his mark as a witty, prolific journalist. He was also noted for his prodigious drinking and an extravagance that landed him several times in debtors' prison. By the time Thackeray came across him he was, in the words of another friend, 'a ruin, a glorious ruin nevertheless'. That same friend penned a memorable description of Maginn at the end of his life, when he was living in poverty in Walton-on-Thames. 'He was quite emaciated and worn away; his hands thin, and very little flesh on his face; his eyes appeared brighter and larger than usual; and his hair was wild and disordered. He stretched out his hand and saluted me… he lives a rollicking life, and will write you one of his ablest articles, while standing in his shirt, or sipping brandy. We talked on Seneca, Homer, Christ, Plato, and Virgil.'

Theodore Hook is now remembered, if at all, as a prankster. It was Hook who once made a bet with a friend that he could briefly make a nondescript house in Berners Street the most famous address in London. He did so by sending out thousands of letters in the name of the householder, a woman who had offended him, requesting visits and deliveries. Beginning at five in the morning, a dozen chimney sweeps called at the house, followed by an equal number of cake-makers with wedding cakes. As the day progressed, more and more people turned up, summoned by Hook's faked correspondence. Heavily laden coal wagons and vans with pianos on them rumbled along the street. Undertakers arrived with coffins. As one writer reported, 'There were surgeons with their instruments; lawyers with their papers and parchments; and clergymen with their books of devotion. Such a babel was never heard before in London, and to complete the business, who should drive up but the Lord Mayor in his state carriage; the governor of the Bank of England; the chairman of the East India Company; and even a scion of royalty itself, in the person of the Duke of Gloucester.'

Thackeray, a sociable and clubbable man, was himself something of a bohemian, although one who never left his bourgeois comforts too far behind. In his last completed novel, *The Adventures of*

Philip, he provides an unabashedly romantic, even sentimental, eulogy of bohemia as: 'a land over which hangs an endless fog, occasioned by much tobacco; a land of chambers, billiard-rooms, supper-rooms, oysters; a land of song; a land where soda-water flows freely in the morning; a land of tin-dish covers from taverns and frothing porter; a land of lotos-eating (with lots of cayenne pepper), or pulls on the river, of delicious reading of novels, magazines, and saunterings in many studios; a land where men call each other by their Christian names; where most are poor, where almost all are young, and where, if a few oldsters do enter, it is because they have preserved more tenderly and carefully than other folks their youthful spirits, and the delightful capacity to be idle.' He ends with the sad admission that, 'I have lost my way to Bohemia now.'

From the beginning, English bohemianism of the Victorian era was divided between those, like Thackeray, who dabbled in dissipation and those who, either through choice or necessity, lived lives that were both dissolute and (often) near-destitute. The nineteenth century had its own version of Grub Street. In the late 1840s and early 1850s, a group of young journalists and writers emerged, most of them acolytes of either Dickens or Thackeray, who could truly be said to be London bohemians. The most prominent of these was George Augustus Sala, born in 1828, who wrote for Dickens's magazine *Household Words* when he was in his early twenties and went on to a long and intermittently very successful career as a novelist, foreign correspondent and occasional pornographer. (He wrote an erotic pantomime entitled *Harlequin Prince Cherrytop and the Good Fairy Fairfuck*, which was privately printed in the 1870s, and *The Mysteries of Verbena House*, or *Miss Bellasis Birched*, a notable example of Victorian spanking literature, has been attributed to him.) In the memoirs he published at the end of his life, Sala wrote of 'the dark days of the long nightmare of Bohemianism', but, throughout his twenties and well into middle age, he could be considered, as he admitted

GEORGE AUGUSTUS HENRY SALA PHOTOGRAPHED BY MATHEW BRADY,
BETWEEN 1855 AND 1865

in another context, an 'ultra-Bohemian'. He was a prodigious boozer. 'In his young days,' according to a publisher who wrote from bitter experience, 'when he got on the spree, he was as likely to be unfit for work for weeks as days.' He was also completely unreliable when it came to money. In an 1855 letter to his friend and fellow journalist Edmund Yates, he admits to owing Yates £2 while begging for a loan of a further £5 and acknowledging that the return of the money will be 'problematical'.

There were plenty of others like Sala. They gathered in Fleet Street pubs like Ye Olde Cheshire Cheese and the Cock

Tavern. The brothers Robert and William Brough moved to London from the North West in 1848 and threw themselves into hectic careers as literary jacks-of-all-trades. Both produced a vast amount of work in a short period of time, much of it for the stage, and both died young. Scotsman Angus Reach, born in Inverness, was a parliamentary reporter before he was 21 and went on to produce pioneering journalism about the lives of the poor in the manufacturing districts of Lancashire and Yorkshire. His less serious works included *The Natural History of Bores* and a comic novel entitled *A Romance of a Mince Pie*. James Hannay had embarked on a naval career, but had been court-martialled and thrown out of the service for drunkenness and insubordination when he was still in his teens. He went on to a hand-to-mouth life as a journalist and author of nautical novels. Of a slightly older generation were the Mayhew brothers, Henry and Augustus. Henry was a writer and experimenter in chemistry who had once been ejected from his attic lodgings in St Martin-in-the-Fields for using his landlady's stew-pan in an unsuccessful attempt to manufacture diamonds. Like Hannay, he had served as a midshipman (on an East India Company ship rather than in the Royal Navy) and returned to land to a debt-filled career as a freelance journalist. His younger brother Gus wrote both fiction (some of it in collaboration with Henry) and stage farces with titles like *Christmas Boxes* and *The Goose and the Golden Eggs*. Many of these writers had links with radical and republican movements. Many of them wrote for the comic papers which proliferated at the time. *Punch*, soon to become a bastion of Victorian respectability, began as a much more radical journal. Its founders included Henry Mayhew and it featured many of the bohemians as contributors. Several rival comic journals, with names like *Pasquin* and *Man in the Moon*, sprang briefly into life in the 1840s and 1850s.

In the wake of Thackeray's *Pendennis*, a string of lesser novels about literary apprenticeship appeared in the 1850s. Not one is still read today, except by the occasional specialist in minor Victorian literature, although Robert Brough's *Marston Lynch* is interesting in its evocation of the world in which the first London bohemians lived. Unlike Thackeray, with his rose-tinted nostalgia, Brough is surprisingly scathing about bohemia. Its inhabitants, he writes, 'may be characterised generally as men with high artistic or literary aspirations who cannot succeed in life. The causes of their non-success may be infinite. The Bohemian may be indolent, or vicious, or ignorant, or simply incapable.' 'I have lived and suffered in Bohemia,' Brough concludes, 'and, I thank heaven, have escaped from it so long ago as to be able to speak of its miseries, which no longer afflict me, without undue bitterness; and of its joys, which no longer tempt me, without partial fondness.' Brough was still in his twenties when he wrote that and he was to die at the age of 32, his serial novel still unfinished. (It was completed and seen into print by Sala which was appropriate since Brough had only started it because Sala had decamped to Paris on a booze-fuelled excursion without fulfilling a commitment to produce a story for a magazine edited by Edmund Yates. Brough stepped into the breach at the last moment.) Many of the other bohemians of his era died young and their novels mostly died with them. The most lasting work by these writers is the kind of investigative journalism pioneered by Sala, Reach and, most famously, by Henry Mayhew, whose multi-volume *London Labour and the London Poor*, which had first appeared in articles in the *Morning Chronicle*, provided an extraordinary collective portrait of the working people of London.

The Pre-Raphaelites

At much the same time as Sala and the Broughs were taking their first steps in the literary world and carousing in Fleet Street, a very different kind of bohemianism was in evidence in Bloomsbury and Chelsea. The Pre-Raphaelite Brotherhood had been created in 1848 when three young painters, William Holman Hunt, John Everett Millais and Dante Gabriel Rossetti, met together at the Millais family home in Gower Street to draw up a manifesto which was to revolutionise English art. Holman Hunt, the son of a London warehouse manager, began his working life as an office clerk, but was accepted at the Royal Academy Schools in 1844, when he was 17 years old. There he met Millais, two years younger than he was, a child prodigy who had entered the art school at the age of 11. Rossetti, who was also studying at the Royal Academy Schools, proved, in many ways, the dominant figure in the new movement. Both painter and poet, Rossetti was born in London into a family of Italian exiles. His father, himself a poet, had been forced to flee his native country because of his support for Italian nationalism; his mother was the sister of John Polidori, who had been Byron's doctor and the author of one of the earliest of all vampire stories.

The young painters aimed for a simplicity of subject-matter and technique in art which they believed had been lost as early as the sixteenth century (hence their name – Pre-Raphaelite) and issued a set of four declarations of their goals. In addition to a general commitment to study nature and produce good work, expressing genuine ideas, they stated their sympathies with 'what is direct and serious and heartfelt in previous art, to the exclusion of what is conventional and self-parading and learned by rote'. Today, when their work seems so archetypally representative of Victorian art, it is difficult to appreciate how much of a stir the early paintings of the Pre-Raphaelites caused. In 1850, Millais's *Christ in the House of His Parents* proved particularly controversial. Many viewers were appalled and dismayed by it. Dickens, in a review, described Jesus as 'a hideous, wry-necked, blubbering, red-headed boy, in a bed-gown, who appears to have received a poke in the hand, from the stick of another boy with whom he has been playing in an adjacent gutter'. Mary was 'so horrible in her ugliness, that... she would stand out from the rest of the company as a Monster, in the vilest cabaret in France, or the lowest ginshop in England'. Although they looked back to an idealised past, the Pre-Raphaelites were the avant-garde of their day, and were vilified by those with more conventional tastes.

Their heyday lasted only a few years. By the mid-1850s the group had effectively disbanded, although their influence was to continue for decades. Rossetti, whose painting *The Annunciation* had attracted reviews almost as vicious as Millais's work, withdrew almost entirely from exhibiting his work in public. He did, however, continue to paint. A milliner's assistant from Southwark named Lizzie Siddal became his principal model, muse and (eventually) wife. She died – possibly from tuberculosis, possibly as a result of laudanum addiction – in 1862 and was buried in Highgate Cemetery, with the only copies of some of her husband's unpublished poems interred in the coffin with her. Seven years later, Rossetti had her body exhumed in order to recover his manuscripts. (He was encouraged in this bizarre act of disinterment by the sinister Charles Augustus Howell, an art dealer, blackmailer and conman whom Swinburne described as 'the vilest wretch I ever came across'. In the 1890s Howell was found dead, his throat cut, in the gutter outside a Chelsea pub.)

As Holman Hunt became increasingly obsessed by religion and Millais embraced the kind of respectability and artistic commissions which were to make him one of the most popular (and occasionally most saccharine) of Victorian painters, Rossetti grew ever more eccentric and bohemian in his habits. After the death of his wife, Rossetti moved to 16 Cheyne Walk and lived there until his death in 1882. Looked after by Fanny Cornforth, a working-class woman who was his model, mistress and housekeeper, he was increasingly dependent on alcohol and laudanum. His Chelsea residence became one of the oddest households in London, which, in addition to its exotic human members, was also home to a small menagerie of unusual animals. At various times, Rossetti

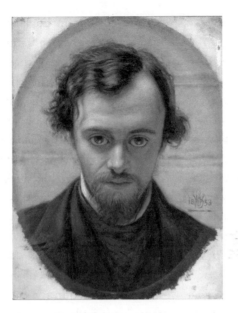

PORTRAIT OF DANTE GABRIEL ROSSETTI AT 22 YEARS OF AGE
BY WILLIAM HOLMAN HUNT, 1882-1883

shared it with kangaroos and wallabies, an armadillo, a zebu, a Japanese salamander and a toucan, which he dressed in a cowboy's hat and trained to ride around the dining-room on the back of a llama. His favourite creature was the wombat and his personal zoo included two of them, supplied to him by Jamrach's, a dealer in exotic wildlife located on the Ratcliffe Highway. A pen drawing by Rossetti in the British Museum shows him weeping into a large handkerchief whilst crouched beside the defunct body of one of his wombats, its legs in the air.

For just over a year, Rossetti shared his home in Cheyne Walk with another exotic creature – the poet Algernon Charles Swinburne. The son of an admiral, Swinburne was educated at Eton and Oxford, and, as a young man, was drawn into the Pre-Raphaelite circle surrounding Rossetti. He gained notoriety with the publication of *Poems and Ballads* in 1866, a collection in which themes of moral and spiritual rebellion combined with a flirtation with the sadistic and sexually ambivalent to create a mixture that was a little too rich for conventional Victorian taste. Many readers, particularly the young, loved it but Swinburne and his poetry were attacked in ways that now seem ludicrously over the top, condemned as 'vile' and full of 'unspeakable foulnesses'. The magazine *Punch*, already established as the home of both respectable middle-class humour and painfully convoluted wordplay, suggested that he should change his name to what it said was the more appropriate 'Swineborn'. Thomas Carlyle called him 'a man standing up to his neck in a cesspool and adding to it' and another critic memorably accused him of being 'the libidinous laureate of a pack of satyrs'. Had these writers known of Swinburne's pornographic writings, hidden from all but a few close friends, they would doubtless have been apoplectic. The poet wrote a salacious play called *La Soeur de la Reine*, in which Queen Victoria has affairs with her prime ministers and one with William Wordsworth, who introduces her to 'nameless practices' that delight her. She also has an unacknowledged sister working as a prostitute in the Haymarket and courtiers who rejoice in the names of the Duchess of Fuckingstone, Sarah Butterbottom and Molly Poke.

In life as in literature, Swinburne was calculated to drive the respectable to distraction. Before 1879, when he moved to Putney to enjoy the more sedate, suburban pleasures of sharing a villa with his friend and admirer Theodore Watts-Dunton, he was a heavy drinker. At one club a series of drunken nights culminated in an occasion when, too puddled by booze to find his own hat on leaving, he tried those of other members. One by one, each of these proved too small for his head, so one by one he threw them to the ground and stamped on them. This was not the behaviour expected of a Victorian gentleman and Swinburne was banned from the club. His sexual interests lay chiefly in flagellation and he regularly paid upmarket prostitutes in St John's Wood to beat him. In 1867, Rossetti

SKETCHED PORTRAIT OF 23-YEAR-OLD ALGERNON CHARLES SWINBURNE
BY DANTE GABRIEL ROSSETTI, 1860

gave the American actress Adah Menken ten pounds to seduce Swinburne, who had never actually slept with a woman, but she was obliged to return it, telling Rossetti that she had failed and that, 'I can't make him understand that biting's no good.' Swinburne, ever mischievous, did not help his reputation by deliberately spreading stories, almost certainly untrue, about the extent of his own depravity. The most extravagant was that he had had sex with a pet monkey, which he had then killed, grilled and eaten.

The Aesthetes

Rossetti and Swinburne were amongst the precursors of the Aesthetic Movement, the championing of the idea of 'art for art's sake', which began to emerge as a cultural force in the 1860s and 1870s, taking as its founding texts works by the Oxford academic

Walter Pater, with their emphasis on the importance of beauty and intensity of experience. By the 1880s, aestheticism was at its peak and exemplified by two men – one Irish, one American and both masters of self-promotion. The young Oscar Wilde was then at the beginning of the career that was to lead him from gilded fame to outcast notoriety. Although he had published a volume of poetry and worked as a literary journalist, he was already as well known as a personality as he was for his art. 'I have nothing to declare but my genius,' he is supposed to have said when arriving in America on a lecture tour in 1882 and he spent much of the following decade endeavouring to persuade the British public that he had been right to make the remark. He was soon one of the most familiar figures in the cultural landscape of the country.

Born in Massachusetts, the son of an engineer, James McNeill Whistler was 20 years older than Wilde and already established as a successful, if controversial, artist. As a young man he had attended West Point as a military cadet, but, deciding he wanted to be an artist rather than a soldier, he left the USA for Europe. He studied in Paris, where he imbibed the spirit of bohemia and admired the work of avant-garde artists such as Courbet. He moved to London in 1859, where his reputation grew both as a painter and a wit whose provocative remarks were as well known as his views of the Thames and his portrait of his mother. Not everyone liked his work. In 1887, the critic and grand cultural panjandrum John Ruskin wrote of one of Whistler's paintings that, 'I never expected to hear a coxcomb ask two hundred guineas for flinging a pot of paint in the public's face.' The artist was outraged and sued Ruskin for libel. After a lengthy trial, Whistler won his case in court, but was awarded only a farthing's damages by the judge. He retained his self-assurance and bowed to no one in his admiration of his own talents. When a gushing female enthusiast remarked, 'I only know of two painters in the world, yourself and Velasquez,' Whistler's response was immediate. 'Why drag in Velasquez?' he asked.

PORTRAIT OF JAMES ABBOTT McNEILL WHISTLER
BY WILLIAM MERRITT CHASE, 1885

Punch was swift to seize upon the comic possibilities of the movement and, beginning in 1880, caricatures of the great poet Jellaby Postlethwaite and the painters Pilcox and Maudle began to appear regularly in its pages. (Ironically, these were the work of the cartoonist George du Maurier, whose novel *Trilby*, as we shall see, was later responsible for propagating his own vision of the bohemian life.) These aesthetes are shown as ludicrously affected characters, fit only to be mocked by sensible members of society. Postlethwaite sits in a café, contemplating a lily in a glass of water, and tells the waiter he is in no need of further sustenance; Maudle, when told by a mother that her son wishes to be an artist, can only reply, 'Why should he be anything? Why not let him remain for ever content to exist beautifully?'

Probably the most memorable satire of the Aesthetic Movement was *Patience*, Gilbert and Sullivan's comic opera of 1881, in which the 'Fleshly Poet' Bunthorne is the adored object of affection for 20 lovesick maidens. Bunthorne, of course, turns out to be a sham, who has merely adopted the persona of an aesthete because of 'a morbid love of admiration'. In one of his solo songs, he reveals what you should do 'if you're anxious for to shine in the high aesthetic line'.

'You must,' he says, 'lie upon the daisies/And discourse in novel phrases/Of your complicated state of mind' and you should remember that, 'You will rank as an apostle in the high aesthetic band/If you walk down Piccadilly with a poppy or a lily in your medieval hand.' In one sense, Gilbert's lyrics express the kind of hearty English philistinism that the aesthetes disliked so much; in another, they reflect a perfectly reasonable disdain for pretension and hypocrisy. They are also very funny. One of the models for Bunthorne was Oscar Wilde. Another, it is clear from photographs of the actor George Grossmith in the role, was Whistler.

Punch and Gilbert and Sullivan were merely reflecting the prejudices of the average middle-class man and woman. Artistic bohemia, as represented by the likes of Wilde and Whistler, was also associated in the public mind with other eccentric movements that affronted the common sense of bourgeois Victorians. The Society for Rational Dress, founded in 1881, campaigned for women to be liberated from the need to wear confining clothing such as tight corsets and vast, unwieldy skirts. Almost immediately it attracted the ridicule of *Punch* cartoonists and versifiers, who poked fun at 'dresses quite worthy a modern burlesque/With garments for walking, and tennis, and talking/All terribly manful and too trouseresque!' The same decade saw growing interest in the teachings of the German naturalist Gustav Jäger, who advocated, for supposed health reasons, the wearing of animal fibres such as wool, rather than plant fibres like cotton, close to the skin. Jäger's ideas inspired the creation of the Jaeger clothing firm in 1884 (still existing today) and high-profile disciples like George Bernard Shaw promulgated them, but they were seen by most contemporaries as cranky and not quite proper. So too was vegetarianism, which grew in popularity during the century. The Vegetarian Society was founded in 1847 and had nearly 5,000 members by the 1890s, but abstaining from the eating of meat was still seen as faddish. Its advocates risked ridicule as much as the 'fleshly poets' who inspired Bunthorne.

At the same time that the upper middle-class bohemia of the aesthetes flourished, some poets and painters in London were living lives that were not so much bohemian as near-destitute. Francis Thompson was born in Preston, the son of a doctor. He half-heartedly studied medicine himself, but his real interest was poetry and he moved to London in 1885, hoping to make his mark in the literary world. Instead he ended up living rough on the streets, an opium addict whose only income came from selling matches and begging from passers-by. Close to suicide, he later claimed he was saved from self-destruction by a vision of his eighteenth-century predecessor in despair, Thomas Chatterton. He was finally rescued from penury when he sent some poems to an Anglo-Catholic magazine called *Merry England*. The husband and wife editors of the magazine, Wilfrid and Alice Meynell, recognised Thompson's talents and took him under their wings, providing him with a home and arranging for the publication of his first book of poetry in 1893. Sadly, his health had been irrevocably undermined by his addiction and his life on the streets. His last years were plagued by illness and he died of tuberculosis in a Catholic hospital in St John's Wood in 1907, aged 47. Posterity has not treated Thompson much better than his contemporaries did and his brand of intense Catholic mysticism, exemplified by his best-known work, 'The Hound of Heaven', has not proved lastingly popular. He has even suffered the posthumous indignity of being proposed as a candidate for the role of Jack the Ripper, although the identification of him with the Whitechapel killer seems, at best, extremely improbable. It's kinder, and more sensible, to remember Thompson, a great lover of cricket, as the author of 'At Lord's', a wonderfully nostalgic evocation of two sporting heroes from his boyhood.

Chapter Three

1890s BOHEMIA

'It's fang de seeaycle *that does it, my dear,*
and education, and reading French'
Mrs Scamler in JOHN DAVIDSON, *Earl Lavender*

Aubrey Beardsley and The Yellow Book

THE JOURNALISTS' BOHEMIA inhabited by the
likes of George Augustus Sala and the Brough brothers in
the 1850s was still flourishing later in the century. (Sala himself did
not die until 1895.) There was also the *milieu* which is depressingly
reflected in George Gissing's autobiographical novel, *New Grub
Street*, first published in 1891. The two central characters of
the novel stand at each end of the literary spectrum as Gissing
envisages it. Edward Reardon, clearly a version of Gissing himself,
is a fine writer but he is hampered by poverty and by marriage
to a woman who cannot sympathise with his art. Jasper Milvain
is a glib and facile reviewer with his eye firmly set on worldly
success. As the novel unfolds, we watch Milvain's inexorable rise
and Reardon's equally inevitable downfall. Gissing knew well the
poverty and misery of late Victorian London which he evoked
so brilliantly in his novels. A classical scholar whose academic

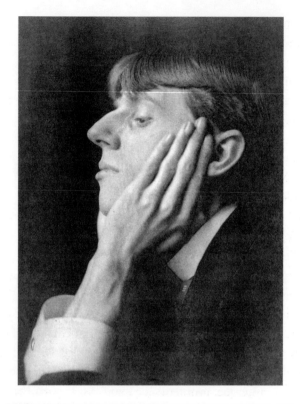

PORTRAIT OF AUBREY BEARDSLEY BY FREDERICK H. EVANS, 1895

career was ruined when he was imprisoned briefly as a young man for theft, he became a prolific novelist, but it was only towards the end of his life that he began to earn enough to free him from haunting financial anxieties.

However, there was also a new, effete *fin-de-siècle* bohemianism which both Sala and his rumbustious successors and Gissing's impoverished toilers at the literary coalface would have had difficulty recognising. This is the 1890s London bohemia that is best remembered today. Its most characteristic inhabitant was Aubrey Beardsley. In some senses, Beardsley was not always sympathetic to the bohemians of his era. He disliked Ernest

Dowson for his drunkenness and loutish behaviour under the influence of liquor, and admired dandyism more than dissipation. 'The more society relaxes the less charm and point there is in Bohemianism,' he once wrote in a letter to his actress sister Mabel and went on to remark waspishly that it 'will never quite die in England as it is the refuge and consolation of the unsuccessful.' However, although Beardsley's life and career were brief and cut short by tuberculosis, he was one of the defining figures of his age. When Max Beerbohm claimed, in 1896, that he belonged 'to the Beardsley period', he was only half in jest.

Aubrey Vincent Beardsley was born in Brighton in 1872 and went to school there. He began his working life in an architect's office, but, although he had very little formal training in art, his extraordinary talent as a black-and-white illustrator was soon recognised. His first important commission came in 1893 from the publishing firm of JM Dent & Sons, which invited him to provide illustrations for an edition of Malory's *Le Morte d'Arthur*. Notoriety came the following year with his drawings for Oscar Wilde's *Salome* which were condemned by a critic in *The Times* as 'fantastic, grotesque, unintelligible for the most part and, so far as they are intelligible, repulsive.'

Beardsley could be whimsically disparaging of his own gifts. 'I make a blot upon the paper,' he once told WB Yeats, 'and begin to shove the ink about and something comes.' In reality, he had a firm sense of his genius and an acute awareness that his time to display it was likely to be short. He had been diagnosed with tuberculosis as a boy and his brief life as an artist was punctuated by long periods when he was too ill to work. Despite his condition, he produced an astonishingly rich body of work in the space of no more than a few years. In his final months he became a convert to Roman Catholicism and began to worry about what he saw as the immorality of some of it. The thought of his illustrations for a proposed edition of Aristophanes's Ancient Greek comedy

Lysistrata, which included nudity, farting and a number of giant erections, particularly distressed him. In a last, despairing letter to his publisher Leonard Smithers, written, as he subscribed it, 'in my death agony', he implored him to 'destroy *all* copies of Lysistrata & bad drawings... By all that is holy – *all* obscene drawings.' In March 1898, he died in the French Riviera resort of Menton, where he had settled in the hope of easing his tubercular lungs. He was 25 years old.

Beardsley's name was (and is) inextricably linked with two magazines that embody the spirit of the 1890s. The first was *The Yellow Book*. He was its arts editor for its first four numbers; the literary editor was Henry Harland, an American novelist who had moved to London in 1889. The contributors to the magazine were a mixed bunch. There were the usual suspects from the decadent nineties, such as Ernest Dowson, Max Beerbohm and Lionel Johnson. Several stories by the extraordinary fantasist Frederick Rolfe, otherwise known as Baron Corvo, a title he claimed he had been granted by an Italian noblewoman, were published. (Rolfe, a Catholic convert, went on to publish the novel *Hadrian the Seventh*, a strange narrative of wish fulfilment in which an obscure Englishman, bearing a remarkable resemblance to the author himself, is elected Pope. He was gay and moved to Venice, from where he despatched semi-pornographic letters back to England, supposedly recounting his erotic encounters. If these are to be believed, he was, in the words of his first biographer, leading a life 'compared with which Nero's was innocent, praiseworthy and unexciting'.) The names of more unexpected writers, many of them decidedly unbohemian, can also be found on the contents pages of *The Yellow Book*. Henry James and Kenneth Grahame, John Buchan and Arnold Bennett were all contributors. And then there are the obscure, forgotten figures like the gay poet Charles Dalmon, who once expressed an ambition to meet his end 'crushed to death between the thighs of a guardsman', and

VOLUMES I AND II OF *THE YELLOW BOOK*, 1894

Theodore Wratislaw, a hereditary Count of the Holy Roman Empire, who wrote decadent verse about vampiric women and epicene young men while living a conventional life as a solicitor working at Somerset House.

It was Beardsley, however, who attracted much of the attention, most of it unfriendly. In *The Westminster Gazette*, writing about the artist's drawings for the first issue, a journalist suggested that 'we do not know that anything would meet the case except a short Act of Parliament to make this kind of thing illegal'. This was only a taste of things to come. Beardsley was to face a barrage of criticism for the rest of his short life. One critic, later a supporter of his work, described it in 1895 as 'sexless' and 'unclean'. In a witty riposte, Beardsley wrote a letter to the magazine in which the criticism had appeared, stating that, 'as to my uncleanliness, I do the best for it in my morning bath and if [your critic] has really any doubts as to my sex, he may come and see me take it'. *Punch*, of course, as the embodiment of middle-class cultural values, had fun mocking the pretensions of the decadents in a satirical article supposedly written by 'Max Mereboom' and illustrated with a drawing by 'Daubaway Weirdsley' (actually Linley Sambourne, one of the magazine's best-known political cartoonists).

The other shop window for Beardsley's artistic wares was *The Savoy*. Together with *The Yellow Book* it was one of what the critic Holbrook Jackson called 'the favourite lamps around which the most bizarre moths of the Nineties clustered'. Beardsley's work featured heavily in *The Savoy* – the first issue, which appeared in January 1896, not only included his illustrations, but also a poem and the beginnings of his never-finished novel *Under the Hill*. This erotic tale, expurgated so as to make it publishable in the magazine, has been called 'one of the great creative achievements of the period' by Beardsley's biographer Stanley Weintraub, but the author's contemporaries were not so generous. According to the journalist and critic Haldane Macfall, it was 'fantastic drivel, without cohesion, without sense, devoid of art as of meaning – a sheer, laboured stupidity, revealing nothing – a posset, a poultice of affectations'.

The Savoy's publisher was Leonard Smithers, a man described by Oscar Wilde as the 'most learned erotomaniac in Europe', which might be construed as a high-flown way of acknowledging that he was a pornographer. (Wilde also joked that Smithers produced editions of three copies – 'one for the author, one for yourself, and one for the police'.) Born in Sheffield, Smithers began his working life in the law, but he turned to publishing and bookselling as a young man. As a publisher, he produced editions of upmarket erotica in collaboration with Sir Richard Burton, the explorer, traveller and translator of *The Book of One Thousand and One Nights*. He moved on to even racier material with a succession of erotic novels and published two volumes of poetry by the occultist Aleister Crowley, one of which, the suggestively titled *White Stains*, included verses on pederasty and necrophilia. As a bookseller, Smithers had a shop in the ultra-respectable Royal

Arcade, Old Bond Street, and a discreet sideline in selling erotica and curiosa via catalogue. Amongst the oddest books he ever offered for sale was an edition of Thomas à Kempis's *The Imitation of Christ*, bound in human skin. Describing it in his catalogue notes as a 'gruesome curiosity', he went on to note that it was 'the only example of human skin binding that has been offered for sale for many years past' since 'owing to the severe restrictions of the medical schools, and the prejudices of medical men, it is extremely difficult to obtain any portion of dead humanity'.

Yet Smithers was far from being just a seedy pornographer or specialist in bizarre book-bindings. He deserves credit for his contributions to the culture of the 1890s. Not only did he launch *The Savoy*, he was also prepared to publish Oscar Wilde in the years after the playwright's trial and disgrace. *The Ballad of Reading Gaol* appeared under Smithers' imprint and so too did editions of *An Ideal Husband* and *The Importance of Being Earnest*, although without Wilde's incriminating name attached to them. His illustrated books included work by Charles Conder, who once ungratefully remarked that Smithers had a face like 'the death mask of Nero', and the first collection of caricatures by Max Beerbohm. He published verse by Ernest Dowson, Lord Alfred Douglas and Arthur Symons, the literary editor of *The Savoy* and another characteristic 1890s figure.

Although not an obviously attractive man, Smithers was a great womaniser. He 'had mistresses all over London', fellow publisher Grant Richards once noted. 'He chose them for the neighbourhoods in which they lived, that, wherever he was, he might always find company – in much the same spirit as that in which the Postmaster-General sprinkles post offices throughout the length and breadth of London.' He was also a heavy drinker and a chloral addict, and he met a strange end in 1907, when his naked body was discovered in a house near Parson's Green surrounded by dozens of empty bottles of Dr Collis Browne's Chlorodyne.

The Café Royal

According to the editors of a 1990 anthology of writings on bohemia, there are only two elements of bohemianism, in all corners of the world, which are ever-present. One is an attitude of dissent to the prevailing values of middle-class society. The other is a café. For nearly a century *the* café for London bohemianism was the Café Royal in Regent Street. It was established in 1865 by a Frenchman, Daniel Nicholas Thévenon, who had fled Paris to evade his creditors, changed his name to Daniel Nicols and decided (rightly, as it turned out) that opening a café in the West End was his route to fame and fortune. Initially much of his business came from fellow French exiles, but word of the Café Royal's superb food, wine cellar and ambience soon spread. By the 1890s its customers included most of the writers and artists best remembered from the period. The Domino Room in the Café, with its marble-topped table, plush velvet benches and gilded mirrors, was filled with poets, painters, actors, journalists and musicians. Before his downfall, Oscar Wilde was a regular visitor, often in the company of Lord Alfred Douglas, and he once became so elevated by the absinthe he had imbibed that he began to hallucinate, thinking that he was in a field of tulips rather than a café. Max Beerbohm, Aubrey Beardsley and the egregious Frank Harris were others who met in what Arthur Symons called 'a luxurious, convenient, unconventional Café'.

Frank Harris is now a mostly forgotten figure, but, in his heyday in the 1890s, he was one of the most easily recognisable men in literary London. Bernard Shaw once said of him that 'he is neither first rate, nor second rate, nor tenth rate. He is just his horrible unique self.' Born in Ireland, Harris had run away to America when he was little more than a boy and earned his living at various times as a boot black, a building worker on the new Brooklyn Bridge, a cowboy, a hotel manager and the inventor of

THE CAFÉ ROYAL, LONDON, WILLIAM ORPEN, 1912

a pornographic card game called 'Dirty Banshee', which showed pictures of satyrs and goddesses in erotic poses. He returned to Britain in his twenties and talked and blustered his way into a successful career as a journalist, which culminated in his editorship of the *Saturday Review* from 1894 to 1898. A shameless liar, who, according to Max Beerbohm, only told the truth 'when his invention flagged', Harris was an unstoppable monologist who knew everybody who was anybody in the literary world. He commissioned work from Shaw, Wilde, Beerbohm and HG Wells and the Café Royal became virtually his editorial office. It was also the scene of some of the many seductions and sexual encounters he related in his multi-volume autobiography *My Life and Loves*, once deemed so lewd and sensational that it was banned from publication in Britain. Future novelist Enid Bagnold was told by Harris that 'Sex is the gateway to life.' So, she later wrote, 'I went through the gateway in an upper room in the Café Royal.' It was here too that Harris hosted a lunch in which he attempted to persuade Oscar Wilde that he should drop his action for libel against the Marquess of Queensberry and get out of the country. Egged on by his lover Lord Alfred Douglas, who was also present, Wilde dismissed Harris's arguments and decided, with fateful consequences, to press on with his court case.

The Café Royal was at the heart of 1890s London culture and, as we shall see, it continued to play an important role in the capital's artistic life into the 1950s. However, not everyone was impressed by its supposed Continental sophistication and its bohemian ambience. 'If you want to see English people at their most English,' the actor-manager Herbert Beerbohm Tree, half-brother to Max Beerbohm, commented, 'go to the Café Royal where they are trying their hardest to be French.'

Exotic Blooms and Doomed Poets

Strange flowers bloomed (and often enough wilted) in the hothouse atmosphere of 1890s London. Few were stranger than the poet and musician Theo Marzials and the Baltic Swedish aristocrat, poet and short-story writer Count Eric Stenbock. Marzials was the son of the pastor of the French Protestant Church in London. He had first come to literary attention in 1873 as the author of what has since been described as the worst poem in the English language. 'A

Tragedy', with its arresting opening lines ('Death! Plop. The barges down in the river flop. Flop, plop.'), is certainly terrible, although devotees of the great William McGonagall may argue that the Scotsman produced even worse verse than the Anglo-Frenchman. The flamboyant Marzials, 'camp' before the term was invented, worked for a time at the British Museum and once disturbed the tranquillity of the old Reading Room by leaning out of one of its galleries and crying out, 'Am I not the darling of the Reading Room?' to those working below. He was still writing poems in the 1890s and two were published in *The Yellow Book*. Max Beerbohm knew him and described his 'flowing moustaches, long hair and a silk tie that fell in folds over the lapels of his coat'. In later life, Marzials moved to Devon where he subsisted largely on a diet of beetroot slices and Dr Collis Browne's Chlorodyne, to which he had become addicted in his London days. He died in 1920. Marzials is a prime example of those many poets of the day who have ended like Enoch Soames. The subject of a sad, fantastical tale by Beerbohm (who may have been thinking of Marzials as he wrote it), Soames travels to the British Library of the future. He is convinced that it will be full of volumes proclaiming his genius as a poet, but he discovers that the only mention of him is in a scholarly article about a short story by Max Beerbohm. Soames has been forgotten. Perhaps Marzials's fate is crueller. He is very faintly remembered, but only as the writer of an atrociously bad poem for people to mock.

Eric Stenbock was born in Cheltenham in 1860, the son of an English mother and the Count de Bogesund, a Swedish aristocrat with royal connections who was heir to vast tracts of land in Estonia. His father died the year after his son was born and Stenbock grew up in England. He studied at Balliol College, Oxford and his first collection of poems was published when he was still an undergraduate. After inheriting money from his Swedish grandfather, he had no need to earn a living and could indulge his tastes as he wished. Gay and obsessed by the wilder fringes of religion and the occult, he dressed eccentrically for the time (a bright green suit with an orange shirt was a favourite outfit) and became a familiar figure in decadent circles. 'There was in him something fascinating, disconcerting,' the writer Arthur Symons noted, 'the manners of the man might easily have become repulsive; yet, all the same, he might, for all I knew, have strayed out of a wild beast show, without any intention of returning thither. Then, as always, he was one of the most inhuman beings I have ever encountered; inhuman and abnormal; a degenerate, who had I know not how many vices.' Ernest Rhys records a visit to Stenbock's flat in Chelsea where he was greeted by the Count with a toad called Fatima, supposedly his magic 'familiar', perched on one shoulder. In these rooms Stenbock also kept a shrine where the flames of a lamp, sacred to the Count if no one else, burned between a bust of Shelley and an ebony image of the Buddha. Oscar Wilde, calling upon Stenbock out of curiosity because he had heard about his eccentricities, mistook the lamp's purpose and used it to light his cigarette, whereupon the appalled Count promptly fell into a real or (more likely) histrionic swoon. Wilde exited equally promptly, leaving his host stretched out on the carpet. Addicted to both alcohol and opium, Stenbock eventually moved to Brighton to stay with his mother and stepfather Sir Francis Mowatt, but his behaviour was becoming increasingly uncontrollable and violent. He died on 26 April 1895, reportedly as the consequence of a drunken quarrel with Sir Francis, during which, waving a poker in a rage, Stenbock fell over and hit his head on a fireplace grate. He was just 35.

Stenbock was not alone in an early demise. Like rock stars, bohemians (at least in the popular imagination) have a tendency to live fast and die young, and the 1890s provided plenty of examples of creative lives cut short. Aubrey Beardsley, of course, succumbed to tuberculosis at the age of 25. The short-story writer and essayist Hubert Crackanthorpe, whose work was championed by no less a figure than Henry James, was only a year older when he disappeared from his Paris home in 1896. More than a month later his body was pulled from the Seine. Almost certainly, he had committed suicide. He had been living in a curious *ménage à quatre* with his wife Leila, a poet who had published verse in *The Yellow Book*, his mistress, the sister of fellow writer Richard Le Gallienne, and Leila's lover. This had broken up when Leila and the lover had left and she had sued for divorce, claiming 'legal cruelty', which may well have been a euphemism to cover the fact that Crackanthorpe had infected her with a venereal disease. His mistress had departed as well and, facing social disgrace, he could see no way out, but the waters of the Seine. It was also in Paris that the American poet William Theodore Peters, a friend of Ernest Dowson and occasional visitor to meetings of the Rhymers' Club in Ye Olde Cheshire Cheese pub in Fleet Street, achieved an even more archetypally bohemian death by starving to death in a garret.

Garrets were popularly seen as the natural homes for poets of the period. 'The proper writing place is a garret,' Richard Le Gallienne wrote. 'There is an inspiration in skylights and chimneys.' The period was certainly alive with impoverished *poètes maudits* who could afford little more than to rent rooms in the upper storeys of London lodging houses. Lionel Johnson was educated at Winchester and Oxford, and converted to Catholicism in 1891. Throughout the nineties he earned a precarious living from his verse and from literary journalism. Johnson was once described by a friend as looking like 'some old-fashioned child who had strayed by chance into an assembly of men'. He was so slight and boyish in appearance that the critic Edmund Gosse, entertaining a number of literary people at his house, suggested to him that he might like to go and play in the garden, mistaking him for one of his young son's friends. A prodigious drinker, he kept a large jug of whisky on his bookshelf between a volume of Baudelaire and the poems of Walt Whitman, and regularly poured tots from it as he worked.

He died in 1902 at the age of 35. In many accounts his death is said to be the result of falling off a bar stool in a Fleet Street pub. The truth is more mundane and less emblematic of a misspent life. He took a tumble in the streets of the city and died of a stroke as a consequence. Johnson has been largely forgotten today, but some of his finest poems, such as 'By the Statue of King Charles at Charing Cross' and 'The Dark Angel', deserve rediscovery.

John Barlas was an Oxford-educated socialist, an active member of the Marxist Social Democratic Federation in the 1880s, who also published eight books of poetry in the decade between 1884 and 1894. His poetry, which embodies his taste for *fin-de-siècle* decadence rather more than his political ideas, won him little fame, but he gained a certain notoriety in January 1892 when he stood on Westminster Bridge and fired a revolver in the direction of the Houses of Parliament in order to express his contempt for the place. He was arrested and bailed by Oscar Wilde, who was a friend from his Oxford days. Always a difficult and potentially violent man, Barlas began to suffer delusions, believing that agents of the government were out to get him, and he was committed to an asylum in Scotland in 1894. He died there twenty years later.

However, probably the most interesting example of the *poète maudit* in 1890s London was Ernest Dowson. He was born in Lee, Kent, the son of Frederick Dowson, who owned a dry dock in the East End of London, and his wife. Because Frederick suffered from tuberculosis the family travelled widely in Europe in search of healthier climes and Ernest knew France and the Mediterranean from an early age. After a few terms at Oxford, he returned to London to work for his father's business and to embark on the stuttering literary career he sustained until his death. His poetry was published in *The Yellow Book* and *The Savoy*, house magazines of the Decadents. Much of his work was inspired by his obsessive love for a girl named Adelaide Foltinowicz, the daughter of a Polish restaurateur in Soho, who was only 12 years old when

PORTRAIT OF ERNEST DOWSON, 1890s, PHOTOGRAPHER UNKNOWN

they first met. Her marriage to another man, after an ambivalent relationship with Dowson that had lasted throughout her teenage years, was a bitter blow to the poet. Together with the deaths of both his parents, almost certainly by their own hands, it prompted his further decline into drink and despair. He died in Catford at the age of only 32.

Dowson always seemed a doomed figure, even to his contemporaries. His friend WB Yeats once said of him, 'I cannot imagine the world in which he would have succeeded.' Naturally shy and quiet in company, he could be transformed by alcohol into a noisy and belligerent boor, spoiling for a fight he was all too likely to lose. Memoirs of the period are filled with stories of Dowson's drunkenness, and his taste for brawling in pubs. 'Sober,' wrote his fellow 1890s poet Arthur Symons, 'he was the most gentle, in manner the most gentlemanly of men; unselfish to a fault, to the extent of weakness; a delightful companion, charm itself. Under the influence of drink he became almost literally insane, certainly quite irresponsible. He fell into furious and unreasoning passions; a vocabulary unknown to him at other times sprang up like a whirlwind; he seemed always about to commit some act of absurd violence.' His favoured tipple was absinthe, 'the green fairy', noted for its connotations of French decadence and for its alcoholic potency. 'We met at seven,' he wrote of a night out with the actor Charles Goodhart, 'and consumed four absinthes apiece in the Cock till nine. We then went and ate some kidneys – after which two absinthes apiece at the Crown. After which one absinthe apiece at Goodie's club. Total seven absinthes apiece. These had seriously affected us... This morning Goodhart and I were twitching visibly.' Despite his own intermittent poverty, Dowson was unfailingly generous to others when he had money. The journalist Newman Flower describes how, 'He would discover, through the comradeship of drinking, some literary derelict in a wine shop, and give him all the money he had.'

Both drink and his sexual encounters filled him with a guilt which he strove to exorcise in his poetry. Dowson wrote much of his verse in the Cock Tavern in Shaftesbury Avenue, an absinthe in one hand and a pencil stub in the other, the very picture of boozy, impoverished genius. Other favoured haunts included (inevitably) the Café Royal and many of the pubs in the Strand where the bohemian dipsomaniacs whom the novelist Ranger Gull called 'the Stranded Gentry' chose to drink. Unlike the work of many of his contemporaries, which has disappeared into near oblivion, some of Dowson's poems are still read and remembered today. He had a gift for the memorable phrase ('the days of wine and roses', 'gone with the wind'), and 'I cried for madder music and for stronger wine', a line from his most famous poem, could be the motto not only for his generation of bohemians, but for other generations to come.

The Rhymers' Club

Dowson was a member of that archetypal enterprise of 1890s bohemia, The Rhymers' Club. Founded in 1890 by WB Yeats and the Welshman Ernest Rhys, later to be the first editor of the Everyman's Library of classics, this was a loose association of like-minded poets, many of them with Irish or Celtic backgrounds, who began to meet once a month in Ye Olde Cheshire Cheese pub off Fleet Street. They dined downstairs there and then retired upstairs to a poorly lit room where they smoked their pipes, drank their tankards of beer and read and discussed their latest poems. They also met from time to time in the Domino Room at the Café Royal. These were decorous gatherings and the Rhymers were serious men – 'seething with the stern sense of their poetic mission', as one visitor described them – but their number included some who led dissipated and disorganised lives. Not only Dowson, but also Lionel Johnson and the opium-addicted Francis Thompson were members. John Barlas was an occasional visitor to meetings, as was Richard Le Gallienne, a young Liverpool-born poet who dressed ostentatiously in old-fashioned knee-breeches, wore his hair long and had added 'Le' to his original surname several years earlier in an attempt to associate his work with the presumed decadence and artistic daring of the French. Others included the improbably handsome John Gray, reputed to be the model for Wilde's Dorian Gray, Arthur Symons and John Davidson, a prolific Scottish poet, dramatist and literary scholar who suffered from depression and was to end his life in 1909 by throwing himself into the sea off a Cornish cliff. Even Wilde himself was known to put in an appearance at their meetings. 'If we met in a private house, which we did occasionally,' Yeats later recalled, 'Oscar Wilde came. It had been useless to invite him to the Cheshire Cheese, for he hated bohemia.' The most significant member of the club was Yeats himself, that 'wild Irishman who lives on watercress and pemmican, and gets drunk on the smell of whiskey', as his fellow Rhymer Davidson described him, tongue firmly in cheek.

The Rhymers seem today, for the most part, very tame bohemians. WB Yeats once remarked to Arthur Symons, bemoaning their temperance, 'Symons, if we had a tendency to excess, we would be better poets'. He was only half in jest. Symons himself, the Welsh-born advocate of French symbolism, was firmly of the belief that 'for the respectable virtues poetry has but the slightest use', but was hampered in his own search for unrespectability by his innate conservatism. He experimented with hashish, but didn't like it very much and decided that drink 'brought me no pleasures'. Symons called The Rhymers' Club nothing but a gathering where 'young poets, then very young, recited their verses to one another with a desperate and ineffectual attempt to get into tune with the Latin Quarter'. In later years it suited Yeats's purposes to mythologise his own past and hence the poets of the 1890s. In retrospect, in his autobiographical writings, the Rhymers came to seem much more 'mad, bad and dangerous to know' than they really were. It also suited Yeats to draw a line under youthful indiscretions and he chose to present the 1890s as a period of peculiarly decadent behaviour. This had come to an abrupt end with the close of one century and the beginning of another. 'In 1900,' he recollected several decades later, 'everybody got down off his stilts; henceforth nobody drank absinthe with his black coffee; nobody went mad; nobody committed suicide; nobody joined the Catholic church; or if they did I have forgotten.' In truth, of course, nothing was quite so chronologically simple. Occasional meetings of The Rhymers'

PORTRAIT OF WB YEATS, 1890s, PHOTOGRAPHER UNKNOWN

Club took place until 1904 and several of its members who met unfortunate ends (John Davidson and Lionel Johnson, for example) did so in the first decade of the twentieth century rather than the last one of the nineteenth.

One notable aspect of The Rhymers' Club was the complete absence of women in its ranks. It was not that there were not women poets in the 1890s who were as talented as most of its members. There were also one or two who could more than match any of the men for bohemianism. Althea Gyles, for instance, came from a wealthy family in County Waterford, but moved, first to Dublin and then to London, to live in poverty and pursue her art. She knew both Oscar Wilde and WB Yeats who described her as 'a strange red-haired girl, all whose thoughts were set upon painting and poetry, conceived as abstract images… and to these images she sacrificed herself with Asiatic fanaticism'. She had affairs with occultist Aleister Crowley and, disastrously, with the publisher Leonard Smithers, who treated her appallingly. In 1900, Arthur Symons records a meeting with her in a bedsitting room she was renting near Regent's Park. According to Symons, there was nothing in the place 'except five books (one a presentation copy from Oscar Wilde) and one or two fantastic gold ornaments which she used to wear; chloral by her side, and the bed strewn with manuscripts'. Gyles lived on, 'a noble, difficult being who invariably became the despair of those who had helped her', until 1949.

Occult Bohemia

At the same time as he was cautiously carousing with the Rhymers, WB Yeats was also an inhabitant of an occult bohemia that had grown up in the 1880s and 1890s. This was focused on the bizarre organisation known as the Hermetic Order of the Golden Dawn, which was established in 1888. William Wynn Westcott, an eminently respectable Crown Coroner who also happened to be a freemason, interested in Kabbalism, Rosicrucianism and other esoteric traditions, had come into possession of a collection of documents, the so-called Cipher Manuscripts, which contained details of certain magical initiation rituals. According to Westcott, they also contained the address of a woman in Germany, Anna Sprengel, allegedly the love-child of King Ludwig I of Bavaria and the exotic dancer Lola Montez, who was a powerful exponent of Rosicrucian magic in her own country. He wrote to Anna Sprengel and received back from her a letter in which she authorised him to set up an English organisation to propagate the esoteric teachings she followed. Thus was created the Isis-Urania Temple of the Hermetic Order of the Golden Dawn in Charlotte Street, Fitzrovia. Westcott invited two men he knew from already existing Rosicrucian fraternities to join him in the new organisation and they became the Golden Dawn's ruling triumvirate. One was a retired doctor in his sixties named William Robert Woodman; the other was the much younger and more colourful Samuel Liddell Mathers. Mathers had spent long periods in the British Museum studying esoteric magic in all its forms and had published books on the Kabbalah. Although he was born in Hackney and brought up in Bournemouth, he decided that he was descended from the Clan McGregor and took to riding his bicycle through the streets of London in full Highland dress. He spread the rumour that he was the reincarnation of the Scottish king James IV. A devotee of chess, he played matches in which his opponent was allegedly one or other of the pagan gods. Mathers made the moves both for himself and for the god, divining where the deity wanted his pieces to go by telepathy.

The Order soon attracted some interesting adherents. WB Yeats met Mathers when they were both working in the Reading Room of the British Museum and joined the Golden Dawn in 1890, taking as his motto the Latin phrase *'Demon Est Deus Inversus'* ('The Devil Is God Inverted'). Maud Gonne, Yeats's muse, was also a member of the Golden Dawn as were the actress Florence Farr and tea heiress Annie Horniman, later a pioneer of modern drama production. However, the most notorious initiate was the self-styled 'Great Beast', Aleister Crowley. Crowley was born in 1875 in Leamington Spa, Warwickshire, a surprisingly genteel birthplace for a man who was later dubbed by the newspapers 'The Wickedest Man in the World'. ('It has been remarked a strange coincidence,' Crowley later wrote, tongue only partially in cheek, in his autobiography, 'that one small county should have given England her two greatest poets – for one must not forget Shakespeare.') He came from a wealthy family, but one that subscribed to the fundamentalist Christian tenets of the Plymouth Brethren. His whole career could be read as a revolt against the restrictions of his upbringing. After three years at Cambridge, where he devoted far more time to his interests in chess, poetry and mountaineering than he did to his studies, Crowley arrived in London, took a flat in Chancery Lane under the pseudonym of Count Vladimir Svareff because 'I thought it would be fun to observe the reactions of Londoners to a foreign nobleman' and began to dedicate himself to the practice of magic. He was initiated into the Order of the Golden Dawn by Mathers himself in November 1898.

Crowley's original mentor in magic after joining the Golden Dawn was a memorably odd man named Allan Bennett, now best known as one of the early advocates of Buddhism in Britain. Three years older than Crowley, Bennett was then renowned for his ability as a magician. Reportedly he had created a talisman to bring rain which only worked when submerged in water. He had then dropped it down a sewer drain and been unable to recover it. London went on to endure one of the wettest summers on record. In striking contrast to Crowley, Bennett lived a life of sexual chastity. He was, however, an enthusiastic advocate of drugs, convinced that 'there exists a drug whose use will open the gates of the world behind the Veil of Matter'. Crowley progressed rapidly through the various grades in the Golden Dawn hierarchy, although his way of living ruffled the feathers of those in the order who believed that a magician should refrain from drink, drugs and sex in order to keep his mind clear and his soul pure. Crowley abstained from none of the vices. He cheerfully drank like a fish and was prepared to try any drug that came his way. As for sex, he was rumoured to visit the bedrooms of some female members of the Golden Dawn, both in astral and, more scandalously, in physical form. He eventually became the catalyst for the disintegration of the order when his feuds with other members, including Yeats, led to irreconcilable schisms.

ALEISTER CROWLEY IN A HERMETIC ORDER OF THE GOLDEN
DAWN RITUAL AS RESURRECTED OSIRIS, 1899

Crowley's later career as sex magician, occult author, possible spy and tabloid newspaper bogeyman took him around the world, but he was also to become a recurring, if peripheral, figure in London's bohemia for decades to come. He was a regular at the Café Royal for decades. In the early 1930s, he owned what he said was a magical cloak which made him invisible and he took to stalking through the place with it draped around his shoulders, convinced that no one could see him. As one of the waiters there later recalled, 'I'd only been working there for a week when this chap came into the Café wearing funny clothes, stood in the middle of the place and started babbling away in some weird language. Nobody paid him any attention, but I asked the Head Waiter if something should be done, but he told me not to worry – it was just Mr Crowley being invisible again.' As late as the 1940s Dylan Thomas spotted Crowley in the French House in Soho. The Welsh poet was sitting with a friend, doodling and drawing in a notebook, when an old man on the other side of the pub sent the barman across to them, carrying a sheet of paper with (according to Thomas) identical markings on it. Fearful of being drawn into the old magician's spell-making, Thomas insisted on rushing out of the pub immediately. Crowley died nearly penniless in a Hastings boarding-house in 1947. His last words are variously reported to have been either, 'I'm perplexed', or 'Sometimes I hate myself'.

Gay London and the Wilde Trials

There had been a gay subculture in London for centuries. In eighteenth-century slang a gay man was a 'molly' and molly houses – pubs like the Talbot Inn in the Strand and the Three Potters in Cripplegate Without – were the gathering places for homosexuals from all walks of life. The most famous of the molly houses was, as we have seen, Mother Clap's in Holborn. One unfriendly witness, who visited the place in 1725 in order to gather incriminating evidence against its clientele, reported what he saw. 'I found between 40 and 50 men making love to one another,' he stated in a later court case. 'Sometimes they would sit on one another's laps, kissing in a lewd manner, and using their hands indecently. Then they would get up, dance and make curtsies, and mimic the voices of women.' It was not only behind the closed doors of the molly houses that eighteenth-century gays congregated. In 1781, a writer named George Parker noted that men gathered in Birdcage Walk in St James's Park to signal their desires to one another. 'If one of them sits on a bench, he pats the backs of his hands; if you follow them, they put a white handkerchief thro' the skirts of their coat, and wave it to and fro.' Following mutual recognition of this sexual semaphore, 'they retire to satisfy a passion too horrible for description, too detestable for language'.

Given the state of the law and public opinion, gay men were forced to live in a necessarily hidden world, but, throughout the nineteenth century, a succession of scandals and court cases continued to throw temporary light on it. The White Swan in Vere Street was a Regency 'molly house'. In 1810, it was raided by Bow Street Runners and more than 20 men were arrested. A number were put on trial. Six were put in the pillory, where they were subjected to severe mistreatment by the mob, pelted with mud, offal, dead animals and excrement. Two were hanged.

Sixty years later, in 1871, the trial of Ernest Boulton and Frederick Park had a more benign outcome. The defendants were two androgynous young men who delighted in donning silk and satin dresses to cruise the theatres and arcades of the Strand as 'Stella' and 'Fanny'. At their trial, they were charged with 'conspiring and inciting persons to commit an unnatural offence', one of the witnesses against Boulton describing how he had kissed 'him, she or it' under the impression he was canoodling with a woman. During the six days of the trial, prurient public interest was aroused by the revelation of Boulton's and Park's transvestite lifestyle but the two were eventually acquitted because there was little evidence that men dressing up as women were actually breaking any law.

In 1889, the revelation that a male brothel existed in Cleveland Street where rich and prominent men could pay for the sexual services of working-class boys threw the establishment into a panic. The scandal began with an investigation into a possible theft at the Central Telegraph Office and the questioning of a teenage telegraph boy called Thomas Swinscow. Found with an inexplicably large sum of money on him, Swinscow denied any involvement in theft, but, under pressure, admitted that he had been given the cash in return for sex with a number of men at a house in Cleveland Street which belonged to one Charles Hammond. A police raid on Hammond's house revealed that he had fled the country (presumably he had been forewarned), but several of his accomplices, most importantly another telegraph boy called Henry Newlove, were later taken into custody. Newlove chose to talk and, as he did so, police investigators began to shift uneasily in their chairs. Powerful people were clearly involved. Lord Arthur Somerset, an equerry to the Prince of Wales, was one of those implicated in the scandal and there were even rumours that the Prince of Wales's eldest son, Prince Albert Edward ('Eddy'), had been a visitor to Cleveland Street. Attempts at a cover-up were only partially successful and several upper-class regulars at Hammond's establishment were forced into exile abroad.

As these cases and others showed only too clearly, gays of all classes in the nineteenth century were seen as outsiders, liable to be condemned and punished because of the simple fact of their sexuality. Many chose to hide it; others, particularly artists and writers, decided to be as honest as they could be. Edward Carpenter (1844–1929) was an author, poet, socialist and educator who was an enthusiastic propagandist for most of the progressive causes of the late Victorian era, from rational dress and vegetarianism to living a simple life of self-sufficiency. Perhaps most significantly he was an advocate of gay love. He lived openly with his own lover, a working-class man from Sheffield named George Merrill, for more than 30 years. He published books about sexuality (*Homogenic Love and Its Place in a Free Society, The Intermediate Sex*), which, although some had to be circulated privately to avoid prosecution, had a lasting influence on gay thought.

In the 1890s, at much the same time that Carpenter was formulating his ideas about 'homogenic' love, many of the so-called 'Uranian Poets' were publishing their verse. 'Uranian' – a word derived from classical literature via the work of a German writer named Karl Heinrich Ulrichs to refer to a man sexually attracted to other men – was applied to the work of a number of minor poets active in the period. These included John Gambril Nicholson, a schoolmaster working in north London, the lawyer and journalist Charles Kains Jackson and the Cambridge literary scholar and librarian Charles Edward Sayle. Amongst the magazines that proliferated in the period were several which regularly published 'Uranian' verse. *The Spirit Lamp* was edited for a time by Oscar Wilde's lover Lord Alfred Douglas. *The Artist and Journal of Home Culture* was ostensibly a periodical devoted to the arts and crafts, but, under the editorship of Kains Jackson, became a vehicle for homoerotic poetry and painting. Several of the Uranian poets were connected with a society known as the Order of Chaeronea, founded by a writer and campaigner named George Ives, and (in an indication of its largely upper middle-class and public school-educated membership) named after a Greek battle of the fourth century BC, in which the Sacred Band of Thebes, 150 pairs of male lovers, had fought and died.

The richness of the social and cultural world enjoyed by many of the Uranians and their associates can suggest that it was not too difficult to be both an artist and a homosexual in the nineteenth century. This was not the case. Discretion and a private income could shield an individual, but many people suffered badly from prejudice and stigmatisation when their sexuality was revealed. The life of Simeon Solomon can be seen as an awful example of the dangers of being a gay artist in Victorian Britain. Solomon was born in 1840, the eighth child of a comfortably off Jewish merchant and his wife. He showed talent as an artist from an early age and was introduced to the Pre-Raphaelite circle of Rossetti and Burne-Jones when he was still in his teens. He began to exhibit his paintings at the Royal Academy and elsewhere and seemed set on a successful and prosperous career. His life changed dramatically on 11 February 1873 when he was arrested in a public urinal off Oxford Street and charged the following day with an attempt 'feloniously to commit the abominable crime of buggery'. Found guilty, he spent six weeks in the Clerkenwell House of Detention. A year later, he was arrested in Paris and, charged with a similar offence, was sentenced to three months in a French jail. By the late 1880s, brought low by drink, poverty and social ostracism, Solomon was reduced to selling matches and shoelaces in the street and chalking pictures on the pavement to earn a few pennies. One of his few supporters was the deeply odd Count Eric Stenbock who occasionally advanced him money. He was still capable of remarkable work. The poet Lionel Johnson knew him and wrote to a friend that, 'Simeon Solomon has done me four glorious chalk drawings. The finest, a thing to take your breath away, he did in a state of bestial drunkenness, in my presence: working at it in a sort of frenzy.' Dividing his last years between the street and the workhouse, Solomon died of heart failure in August 1905.

The greatest of all the century's gay *causes célèbres* was, of course, the trial of Oscar Wilde. Born in Dublin in 1854, the son of a famous eye surgeon and his wife, an even more famous poet and ardent Irish nationalist, Oscar Fingal O'Flahertie Wills Wilde excelled as a classicist at Magdalen College, Oxford and first came to public attention in the 1880s as the embodiment of that era's aestheticism. He published poetry and essays, but it was the persona he created that brought him to fame. He was ridiculed in *Punch* as Oscuro Wildegoose and Ossian Wilderness, and, as we have seen, he provided one of the models for the character of Bunthorne in Gilbert and Sullivan's comic opera *Patience*, but for younger acolytes he became the wittiest and most convincing advocate of the new aesthetic philosophy of 'Art for Art's Sake'.

In 1884, he married Constance Lloyd and they had two children in the next two years, but he was rapidly recognising the fact that his primary sexual attraction was to young men. His first male lover was probably the teenage Robbie Ross, 'a saint known in Hagiographia for his extraordinary power, not in resisting, but

SIMEON SOLOMON IN ORIENTAL FANCY COSTUME
PHOTOGRAPHED BY DAVID WILKIE WYNFIELD

in supplying temptation to others', as he described him, who was to prove a loyal friend when disaster struck. However, the great and disastrous love of his life was Lord Alfred Douglas, known as 'Bosie' to family and friends, whom he first met when the poet Lionel Johnson brought the young aristocrat to tea at Wilde's home in Tite Street, Chelsea in June 1891. The son of the ninth Marquess of Queensberry, Bosie was then an undergraduate at Magdalen College, Oxford, Wilde's own alma mater. He was handsome, spoilt, reckless and spendthrift. He wrote poetry and was enthusiastically and unrepentantly gay. By the spring of the following year, he and Wilde, who had long since accepted his desires for young men and acted upon them, had become lovers. They were to remain so for the next three years and their affair was to prove disastrous for them both, but particularly for the older man.

This was the period of Wilde's greatest literary triumphs. His novella *The Picture of Dorian Gray*, first published in *Lippincott's Monthly Magazine* in 1890, met with mixed reviews. Many praised it, but others were swift to condemn. 'It is a tale spawned from the leprous literature of the French Decadents,' a writer in the *Daily Chronicle* loftily and xenophobically opined, before going on to say it was 'heavy with the mephitic odours of moral and spiritual putrefaction'. Another reviewer, in a clear reference to the Cleveland Street Scandal, called it, a tale fit 'for none but outlawed noblemen and perverted telegraph boys'. WH Smith withdrew all copies of the magazine from its railway bookstalls for fear it might pollute the minds of the travelling public. Wilde was soon in a position to care little about bad reviews and booksellers' timidity. In the next few years he became by far the most fashionable and admired playwright in town. His run of box-office hits began with *Lady Windermere's Fan*, first performed at St James's Theatre in February 1892, and continued with *A Woman of No Importance, An Ideal Husband* and, most famously, *The Importance of Being Earnest*.

Throughout the period of his theatrical success, Wilde continued to conduct his increasingly tempestuous relationship with Lord Alfred Douglas, who was a demanding and almost entirely self-centred lover. They regularly quarrelled and made up. They both took other sexual partners and Bosie encouraged Wilde in his increasingly risky encounters with London rent boys. They took holidays together, including one to Algiers, where they indulged in the sexual freedom that tempted well-off Europeans to North Africa, and smoked dope. 'Bosie and I have taken to haschish,' Wilde reported, sounding like some proto-hippie, 'three puffs of smoke and then peace and love.' However, back in London, their affair was attracting unwelcome attention, particularly from the Marquess of Queensberry, Bosie's quarrelsome and half-mad father. Queensberry wrote to his son, forbidding him from seeing the playwright any more. Bosie's response – a telegram which simply read 'What a funny little man you are' – only enraged the Marquess further.

Queensberry's behaviour was rapidly becoming intolerable. Although the lovers did not know this, he was now employing private detectives to build up a portfolio of evidence about Wilde's sex life with young working-class men. On the opening night of *The Importance of Being Earnest*, the Marquess planned to disrupt proceedings by ostentatiously presenting the author with a bouquet of cabbages. Wilde heard in advance of what was being planned and Queensberry was refused admission. The last straw came when Bosie's father left a badly spelled note scribbled on a visiting card at one of Wilde's clubs, addressed to 'Oscar Wilde, posing as somdomite'. Wilde received the note some days later, and decided that enough was enough. 'Bosie's father has left a card at my club with hideous words in it,' he wrote to Robbie Ross. 'I don't see anything now but a criminal prosecution.' Egged on by Bosie, who had always loathed his father, Wilde initiated a private prosecution against Queensberry for libel. It was to prove a terrible miscalculation. Appearing on the witness stand to face questioning from Sir Edward Carson, an old acquaintance from Trinity College, Dublin, Wilde defended himself against the accusation that both his works and his life were immoral with characteristic wit, but Carson's relentless questioning rattled him. In one particularly revealing exchange, the lawyer asked him whether or not he had kissed a certain boy. 'Oh dear, no,' Wilde responded, 'he was a particularly plain boy. He was, unfortunately, extremely ugly.'

It was soon clear that Wilde had no option but to drop the prosecution and Queensberry was found not guilty. It now seemed only a matter of time before the playwright would face charges of sodomy and gross indecency. Friends urged him to flee to France,

OSCAR WILDE PHOTOGRAPHED BY NAPOLEON SARONY, 1882

but it was too late. He was arrested at the Cadogan Hotel in Knightsbridge. (When he was arrested, he was seen to be holding a book with a yellow cover. Although it was actually a French novel, it was immediately assumed to be a copy of *The Yellow Book*, which then suffered by association with the scandal of the day.) Wilde's own trial on a series of counts of gross indecency began on 26 April 1895. During it, Wilde made an eloquent defence of the 'love that dare not speak its name', a phrase taken from one of Bosie's poems. It was, he said, 'such a great affection of an elder for a younger man as there was between David and Jonathan, such as Plato made the very basis of his philosophy, and such as you find in the sonnets of Michelangelo and Shakespeare. It is that deep spiritual affection that is as pure as it is perfect... It is in this century misunderstood, so much misunderstood that it may be described as "the love that dare not speak its name", and on that account of it I am placed where I am now. It is beautiful, it is fine, it is the noblest form of affection. There is nothing unnatural about it.' His words were greeted by spontaneous applause from the public gallery. The jury was unable to reach a verdict and the case, for the moment, collapsed. Released on bail, Wilde took refuge with friends and he may have hoped that the prosecution would now be dropped. Certainly he continued to resist the idea that he should flee the country. 'Everybody wants me to go abroad,' he complained. 'I have just been abroad. One can't keep on going abroad, unless one is a missionary or, what comes to the same thing, a commercial traveller.'

The second trial began on 20 May and lasted seven days. In its course, much the same cast of rent boys and petty blackmailers gave evidence of Wilde's more mercenary sexual activities as had done so in the first trial, but this time his wit and eloquence were largely exhausted. The verdict was predictable. According to the judge, a reactionary figure unlikely to be very sympathetic, Wilde had been 'the centre of a circle of extensive corruption of the most hideous kind among young men' and he was sentenced to two years' hard labour. For a man in his forties who had led a largely sedentary life, this was punishment indeed. He was put on the treadmill and later set to picking oakum. Only when he was transferred from Wandsworth Prison to Reading Gaol did his conditions begin to improve, but first he had to endure further humiliations. During the transfer, he was obliged to stand for a long time, handcuffed and in prison dress, on a platform at Clapham Junction. He was recognised and met with laughter and jeers from a gathering crowd. One man approached him and spat in his face. The regime at Reading eventually proved milder and he was allowed more books and access to writing materials. After his release in 1897, Wilde retired to the Continent, where he led a peripatetic and often impoverished life. He died, of cerebral meningitis, on 30 November 1900, in a cheap Parisian hotel. His last witticism has been reported as, 'My wallpaper and I are fighting a duel to the death. One or other of us has got to go.' More poignantly, he is also said to have remarked during his last days, 'I am dying beyond my means. I can't even afford to die.'

As Yeats recognised when he looked back on the 1890s, Wilde was not naturally a bohemian himself. He may have wished, as he claimed, to 'feast with panthers', but, in his prime, he was happier conversing with duchesses. He enjoyed the good things of life too much to starve in a garret for the sake of his art and he had no need to do so in the years of his artistic and commercial success. It was only the humiliations of his trials, imprisonment and exile that eventually drove him to poverty and a hand-to-mouth existence in Paris. Yet, at his trials, he was inevitably cast as the representative of the bohemian artist – the subversive outsider unwilling to abide by the moral and sexual norms of ordinary society. Wilde's prolonged ordeals in the witness box also alerted Middle England to the existence of a gay subculture in London and suburban man and woman were duly appalled by what was revealed. During his heyday, Wilde had been the licensed jester of late Victorian high society, but his trial and disgrace offered those who prided themselves on their respectability a chance to push bohemia under the carpet. For a short while, it really did seem as if, in the words of the modern critic Hugh David, 'English bohemianism had been tamed and trampled into submission by the overwhelming might of conformity.'

Chapter Four

BOHEMIA 1900–1920

*'Bohemia is only a stage in a man's life, except in the case
of fools and a very few others. It is not a profession'*
ARTHUR RANSOME, *Bohemia in London*

From Trilby *to Arthur Ransome*

A S THE REALITIES of what bohemianism in London
might entail were brought to the public's attention via the
Oscar Wilde trials, it is little surprise that new and less threatening
visions of 'La Vie de Bohème' as lived in Paris were presented to
English audiences in two works of the 1890s and immediately won
enormous popularity. One of these was in George du Maurier's
novel *Trilby* – the story of a virtuous artists' model who falls under
the malign spell of the mesmeric Jewish musician Svengali and is
moulded by him into a great singer. Svengali's name has entered
popular usage to describe someone exercising an unhealthy
influence over another, but much of the novel focuses not on
him, but on the life led by the art students of the Latin Quarter,
who are all in love with Trilby. It's difficult now to appreciate the
impact that this largely forgotten work had on the culture of its

day. The occasional use of Svengali in the language and the name of a hat are all that survive of 'Trilbymania', but, in truth, Trilby was everywhere in the years immediately after its first publication in book form in 1895. It sold by the thousands and was adapted more than once for the stage. There were Trilby waltzes and Trilby dolls, Trilby puzzles and Trilby toothpastes. As a music hall song of 1896 put it, 'We've got Trilby jugs and Trilby mugs and Trilby chairs and lamps/We've all got Trilby plates of meat, and carry Trilby gamps/This Trilby craze will end my days – at home we're all insane/We've Trilby, Trilby, Trilby, Trilby on the brain.' When the craze spread to America there was even a township in Florida which was named Trilby (it still exists). Du Maurier's novel presents an idealised vision of Parisian bohemia, which ultimately derives from *Scènes de la vie de bohème*, filtered through his own experiences as an art student nearly 40 years earlier. Another work of art, which arrived in London two years after the publication of *Trilby*, drew much more directly on Murger's book. Puccini's opera *La Bohème* was given its world premiere in Turin in February 1896 and was first heard in London at the Royal Opera House in October of the following year. It rapidly achieved the popularity and standing in the operatic repertoire that it has retained to the present day.

Bohemia, it seemed, could be tamed if it was firmly located not in London but in Paris where, it was popularly assumed, anything went. It could also be tolerated if it was transformed into little more than the expression of youthful high spirits. Arthur Ransome's *Bohemia in London* was first published in 1907, when its author was in his early twenties. Ransome is now best known for the 'Swallows and Amazons' series of children's books and he may seem an unlikely chronicler of bohemian life, but his career was more varied and adventurous than one might think. He was one of the first to write a literary study of Oscar Wilde. (Published only 12 years after the playwright's death, this involved him in a libel suit brought by the litigious Lord Alfred Douglas which Ransome won.) He was a foreign correspondent in Russia during the years of the Revolution and knew many of the Bolshevik leaders, including Lenin. He met the woman who became his second wife when she was working as a secretary for Trotsky. Nonetheless, Ransome's bohemia is a very gentle one – a world in which 'growing long hair, and refusing to wear a collar' are marks of outrageous rebellion against society's norms, and the worst debauch involves little more than drinking too much red wine in a Soho restaurant. It seems like a pale imitation of earlier bohemian life, filtered through the version seen in *Trilby* and frightened into semi-respectability by the scandal surrounding Oscar Wilde.

There are indeed times when Ransome's evocation of bohemia seems only to be a rose-tinted celebration of the pleasurable irresponsibility of youth. However, it possesses great charm and there is wisdom in his acknowledgement that an elderly bohemian is not always (or even often) to be admired. As he writes, 'There are few sadder sights than an old man without any manners aping the boyishness of his youth without the excuse of its ideals, going from tavern to tavern with the young, talking rubbish till two in the morning, painfully keeping pace with a frivolity in which he has no part... But now, in youth, it is the best life there is, the most joyously, honestly youthful.'

Augustus John and the Slade School Artists

In the 1890s, in parallel to the world inhabited by decadents and outsiders, there still existed the kind of amiable, comfortable, almost exclusively masculine bohemia which Thackeray would have recognised. It was centred on institutions such as the Savage Club, founded in 1857 by a group of journalists and writers, which included George Augustus Sala and the Brough brothers, and was named after the dissolute eighteenth-century poet. There, raffish behaviour and possession of a mistress didn't exclude one from enjoying the benefits of upper middle-class Victorian life. This continued throughout the Edwardian era. It can be glimpsed in a volume like *Mr Punch in Bohemia* of 1910, a collection of prose and cartoons from the magazine that epitomised no-nonsense middle-class ideas. 'Time was,' the anonymous editor reports in his introduction, 'when bohemianism was synonymous with soiled linen and unkempt locks.' The assumption was that this was no longer the case. A man could have his cake and eat it. He could have all the comforts that prosperity brought and yet still congratulate himself on being a bit of a devil at heart.

However, a more 'authentic' bohemianism still flourished. In the years before the First World War nobody epitomised it more than the artist Augustus John, a man to whom legends were attached from an early age. Born in Pembrokeshire in 1878, the son of a solicitor, he was said to have been but an ordinary boy until, during a family holiday, he struck his head on a rock while diving and 'emerged from the water a genius'. By the time he was in his late teens he was already the star of the Slade School of Art, hailed as the greatest draughtsman of his generation, and compared to Michelangelo. At the Slade he showed an early taste for the unconventional, disappearing regularly to the anarchist clubs in the streets off Tottenham Court Road where he sketched such revolutionary celebrities as Louise Michel, the so-called 'Red Virgin' who had fought on the barricades during the Paris Commune, and Prince Peter Kropotkin.

When he left the Slade, John was poised to become an iconic figure in English art and bohemia. As Wyndham Lewis later wrote, 'Here was one who had gigantic earrings, a ferocious red beard, a large angry eye, and who barked beautifully at you from his proud six foot, and, marvellously, was a great artist too. He was reported to like wine, women and song and to be by birth a gypsy.' What

AUGUSTUS JOHN PHOTOGRAPHED BY JACOB HILSDORF, 1909

more was needed to create the perfect bohemian? With his friends
and fellow painters William Orpen and Albert Rothenstein (later
to change his name, too Germanic during the First World War,
to Rutherston), he became a regular at the Café Royal, where he
was to be a familiar face for the next half-century and more. His
first one-man show in 1899 was a success. Still only in his early
twenties, John seemed an enviable figure to fellow bohemians. His
lifelong womanising was only briefly curtailed by marriage to Ida
Nettleship and he soon took up with Dorothy McNeill ('Dorelia'
as she was universally known), who lived in a *ménage à trois* with

the Johns until Ida's early death in 1907. After Ida died, John became obsessed by his own romanticised version of gypsy life. Like Mr Toad in *The Wind in the Willows*, excited by the prospect of the open road, he set off in a blue caravan in the spring of 1909, together with the long-suffering Dorelia and several of their children, to live the Romany dream in the Home Counties. By September, the horses had died, the children had gone down with whooping cough and John had returned to Chelsea.

Throughout the rest of his life John continued to be possessed of most of the tastes of the true bohemian. He was an enthusiastic boozer who was largely instrumental in making pubs such as the Fitzroy Tavern the drinking holes of choice for London's artists and writers. Notoriously promiscuous, he had so many illegitimate offspring that, by the 1930s, he was rumoured to pat the head of every child he met as he walked the streets of Fitzrovia just in case it was one of his. Few women were safe from his advances, although some proved perfectly capable of repelling them if they were unwanted. Viva King describes an occasion when she was reading aloud to him from the works of sexologist Havelock Ellis. She became aware that the painter, aroused by the passage, was emitting strange sounds 'like a sea elephant coming up for air'. 'I realised,' she wrote in her autobiography *The Weeping and the Laughter*, 'it was Augustus starting some "funny business"; but when told to, he returned quietly to his chair.' He was not always so easily rebuffed. Caitlin Macnamara, Dylan Thomas's future wife, reported of John's lovemaking that he 'leaped on her, ripped off her clothes and penetrated her like some mindless hairy goat'.

Augustus John's great rival for the title of King of Bohemia was the American-born sculptor Jacob Epstein. Two years younger than John, he had arrived in London in 1905 and endured a period of extreme poverty (at one point he was sleeping under newspapers rather than blankets in his lodgings) before his work began to gain attention. Not all of the attention was favourable. His nude sculptures for the façade of the BMA head offices (now Zimbabwe House) on the Strand were considered a little too sexually explicit for Edwardian tastes. There were similar problems when he was commissioned to produce a monument to Oscar Wilde for the Père Lachaise Cemetery in Paris. Epstein created a phallic sphinx which upset even the tolerant Parisians and the stone testicles he had sculpted for his figure had to be covered by a butterfly-shaped bronze plaque to avoid offending public decency. The sculptor, infuriated by the alteration to his work, boycotted the unveiling. Some weeks later, Aleister Crowley approached Epstein in the Café Royal. Around the occultist's neck hung a large bronze butterfly. Epstein's monument, complete with testicles, had been returned to its intended state.

The breeding ground for many of these Edwardian bohemians was Augustus John's *alma mater*, the Slade School of Art off Gower Street. 'The Slade continues to produce geniuses,' its principal Henry Tonks once wrote in a letter to a friend, 'we turn them out every year.' Tonks had his tongue firmly in his cheek, but he had a point. Alumni from the Edwardian era included Mark Gertler, Dora Carrington, CRW Nevinson and Stanley Spencer. Many of the male artists, including Gertler, Nevinson and future Vorticist Edward Wadsworth, formed a set which called itself the 'Coster Gang', because its members wore the black jerseys, scarlet mufflers and black hats more usually associated with costermongers. The gang was always up for a fight and, according to Nevinson in his later autobiography, 'We were the terror of Soho and violent participants, for the mere love of a row, at such places as the anti-vivisectionist demonstrations at the "Little Brown Dog" at Battersea. We also fought with the medical students of other hospitals for the possession of Phineas, the bekilted dummy which stood outside a tobacconist's shop in Tottenham Court Road and was... considered the mascot of the University College of London.' One of the least-known and most tragic of the Coster Gang was

John Currie, 'a great painter and a magnificent fellow', according to his friend, the sculptor Henri Gaudier-Brzeska. Currie left his wife and child to live with the model Dolly Henry, but the relationship was a tempestuous one. It ended on 8 October 1914 when Currie shot dead Henry, whom he suspected of posing for pornographic photographs. He then turned the gun on himself. He died in the Chelsea Infirmary three days later. His last words were, 'It was all so ugly'.

A kind of dress code emerged among these art school bohemians. Men wore their hair longer than their non-bohemian contemporaries; women, like Carrington and Dorothy Brett, who were known as the 'Slade Cropheads', chose shorter cuts than were fashionable. The more daring women began to wear trousers; the most avant-garde men divested themselves of theirs and chose to don robes or tunics. Gypsy rings appeared in the ears of both sexes. The place in which to see them in their natural habitat was Chelsea and the high point of their social year became the Chelsea Arts Club Ball. Launched in 1891, and intended from the start to be bohemian in character, the Chelsea Arts Club began its tradition of annual balls with a shindig at the Royal Opera House in 1908. Two years later the ball took place at the Albert Hall, where more than 4,000 people gathered to celebrate Mardi Gras in a riot of colour and crazy costumes, many of them designed by their wearers. Forty female art students joined forces to create an eighty-legged 'Flu Germ' microbe, complete with flashing red lights for eyes. Red devils danced with Sioux chieftains; Romeo and Juliet chatted with a couple of teddy bears, while a man dressed to represent Halley's Comet, a celestial visitor that year, wandered past. 'The fun of it all!' one of those present enthused years later. For decades to come the Chelsea Arts Club Ball was to be the venue where bohemia and the London social season met.

The Café Royal Revisited and Other Clubs

If a ticket to the ball proved unobtainable, a visit to the Café Royal was recommended for those in search of artists at their ease. This continued to be a major centre of the London bohemian universe. In her autobiography, *Tiger Woman*, the model Betty May described, 'the lights, the mirrors, the red plush seats, the eccentrically dressed people, the coffee served in glasses, the pale cloudy absinthes,' and went on to admit, 'I was ravished by all these and felt as if I had strayed by accident into some miraculous Arabian palace… No duck ever took to water, no man to drink, as I to the Café Royal. The colour and the glare, the gaiety and the chatter appealed to something fundamental in my nature…' She took to spending days there, sitting over a single cup of coffee and hoping to be noticed. Her persistence was to be rewarded when Jacob Epstein eventually did just that and invited her to pose for him. It was to be the start of a long career as a bohemian muse.

Epstein and Augustus John were the kings of the café and both had their own bands of admirers and hangers-on who surrounded them whenever they visited. The Café Royal's other habitués included nearly everybody who was anybody in the city's bohemia. Ronald Firbank, the deeply eccentric novelist who provided a literary link between the 1890s and the fiction of Evelyn Waugh and Anthony Powell, was a regular visitor. He was once seen in the Café so drunk on champagne that he had lost his sense of direction and was calmly spreading caviar on his nose rather than on the blinis on his plate. Another familiar face was Horace de Vere Cole, an Irish practical joker who was the driving force behind the so-called Dreadnought Hoax of 1910, in which a number of Bloomsbury pranksters, including Virginia Woolf and Duncan Grant, dressed up as 'Abyssinian' princes and persuaded a Royal Navy captain to give them a tour of his warship.

Peter Warlock, the composer and musicologist, whose real name was Philip Heseltine, was another regular. (He died in Tite Street, Chelsea, probably a suicide, in 1930. His son, born after his father's death, was the art critic Brian Sewell.) Warlock was briefly a close friend of DH Lawrence, but soon fell out with him. 'Heseltine ought to be flushed down a sewer,' Lawrence later opined, 'for he is a simple shit' and he produced a thinly-disguised and unflattering portrait of him as Halliday in *Women in Love*. Warlock retaliated by using an original Lawrence manuscript as toilet paper. He met his future wife (an artists' model known as 'Puma') in the Café Royal, but later turned against the place, calling it 'the very vortex of the cesspool of corruption'. One of Warlock's greatest pals was another composer and writer, Cecil Gray, who, at one time, shared lodgings with him in Battersea. Gray once had a fist fight in the Café with Horace de Vere Cole after he heard Cole deriding the work of Epstein. Both Gray and Heseltine were clearly pugnacious individuals and it was also in the Café Royal that the pair of them ganged up on Edwin Evans, the music critic of the *Daily Mail*, who had the temerity to belittle Béla Bartók, one of their favourite composers. Exchange of insults became exchange of blows and a corner of the Café rapidly became the setting for a free-for-all among a dozen or more individuals. Evans ended up flat on the floor while the Mexican artist Benjamin Corea bounced up and down on his stomach.

TWH Crosland, a visitor to the Café since the 1890s, was a Yorkshire-born author who had been a friend of Lord Arthur Douglas until, like most of Bosie's friends, he fell out with him and was dismissed as 'a brute and more than half a knave'. Crosland would haunt the Domino Room, handing out his visiting card, which had the inscription 'Jobbing Poet' on it and, underneath, the further message, 'Funerals Attended'. When in funds, he would sit for hours in the Café consuming glasses of brandy and milk, working on both poetry and prose, and slowly divesting himself of tie, collar, waistcoat, shirt, socks and shoes until the waiters had to remind him that he could remove nothing more without offending public decency. On one occasion he was sitting in the Café when a mentally troubled man came up behind and half-heartedly struck at him with a knife. After a struggle the man was disarmed and led away. 'The wonder is that Crosland didn't stab *him* in the back,' one of his many enemies remarked when told of the incident.

Eccentrics and bohemians abounded among the Café's clientèle. Alan Odle was a sub-Beardsley illustrator who was remarkable for his long hair, which he coiled around the top of his head. Always unkempt, Odle was said to 'dress like a dustman and carry himself like a duke'. Rudolph Vesey was a wealthy Catholic who threw orgiastic parties which lasted three weeks, the only breaks being when he left them to attend early morning Mass at Westminster Cathedral. Arguably the most extraordinary personality to be seen in the Café Royal at the time was Stewart Gray, a former Edinburgh lawyer who had turned his back on his successful career north of the border to campaign against poverty and unemployment in the English capital. A pioneer of the right to squat, Gray took possession of a large, empty house in Ormonde Terrace, Primrose Hill just before the First World War and threw it open to anyone who fancied taking up residence there. Word of Gray's refuge soon spread to the destitute and the derelict of the city. In the words of Guy Deghy and Keith Waterhouse, in their history of the Café Royal, 'Blind beggars tapped their way there; some came on crutches, others running in case the police were after them; prostitutes rested their walk-weary bones in the attic, where owls had made their nests... mothers fed their children on stairs from which the banisters had been ripped away; and an Indian who said he was a struck-off doctor rocked himself all day on a three-legged chair, humming the same monotonous tune over and over again.' Several artists, including David Bomberg, stayed at Ormonde Terrace for brief periods and the models Betty May and Lilian Shelley both spent time there. Dressed in a ragged selection of mismatched clothes and wearing laceless boots on bare feet, Gray would regularly march into the Café Royal to hawk his strange works of art, painted on scraps of lino and wood, to its more generous customers.

In December 1923, the Café Royal was the scene of a farewell dinner to DH Lawrence who was planning to travel to the USA. At the dinner, his friend, the translator SS Koteliansky, made an emotional speech, expressing his admiration for Lawrence, and smashing a wineglass on the floor at the end of every sentence for emphasis. The novelist himself, usually abstemious, drank too much port, puked over the tablecloth and then passed out. Those members of the party who were still sober were left to pay the bill, tip the waiters generously to clean up the mess, and carry Lawrence off to a house in Heath Street, Hampstead where he was staying and where he promptly threw up again.

Not everybody liked the Café Royal. Writing in 1922, Thomas Burke, author of the once-famous collection of short stories entitled *Limehouse Nights*, found it a grim and inauthentic place, filled with 'young men with pink voices and pink socks fumbling with the arts, and trying to forget that they came from Liverpool'. Burke's jaundiced view of the Café is strongly marked by what would today be called homophobia and he is unpleasantly, if memorably, dismissive of the 'queer creatures' to be found there. 'There sits an hermaphroditic creature with side-whiskers and painted eyelashes,' he wrote, 'praising a soft-bearded youth… There are things in women's clothes that slide cunning eyes upon other women. Male dancers who walk like fugitives from the City of the Plain. Hard-featured ambassadors from Lesbos and Sodom.'

The Café Royal was, of course, long-established, but new haunts also sprang into life in the years before the First World War, often flourishing only briefly and then folding. The Cave of

A NIGHT IN THE CAVE OF THE GOLDEN CALF

the Golden Calf was a basement nightclub and cabaret in Heddon Street (just off Regent Street and now best known as the place where Ziggy Stardust poses with his guitar on the front of David Bowie's 1972 album *The Rise and Fall of Ziggy Stardust and the Spiders from Mars*). It was run by the ex-wife of August Strindberg. Born in Vienna, Frida Uhl had married the Swedish dramatist in 1893 and, soon separated from him, had then embarked on a series of love affairs with writers and poets in her native city. *Persona non grata* in Vienna after an incident in which she fired a pistol during a New Year's party in a smart hotel, she came to London and opened her nightclub on 26 June 1912. The tempestuous Frida was once described as 'the Walking Hell-Bitch of the Western

world' by Augustus John, whom she pursued relentlessly for
months after they had slept together. She twice made theatrical
gestures towards suicide by taking veronal and threatened John
with a revolver on at least one occasion. However melodramatic
and overwrought Frida Strindberg could be, her commitment to
the avant-garde arts was genuine and her nightclub was intended
to provide a refuge and meeting place for the artistically daring.
It was decorated with work by some of the most gifted artists and
sculptors of the period, including Eric Gill, Wyndham Lewis and
Jacob Epstein, much of which disappeared when the club doors
closed for the final time in February 1914. Gill's contribution
included a sculpture of a large, gilded and very evidently male
calf which stood in the heart of the club and gave the place its
name. According to Osbert Sitwell, 'This low-ceilinged nightclub, appropriately sunk below the pavement... and hideously
but relevantly frescoed... appeared in the small hours to be a
super-heated Vorticist garden of gesticulating figures, dancing
and talking, while the rhythms of the primitive forms of ragtime
throbbed through the wide room.'

After the closure of The Cave of the Golden Calf, Frida
Strindberg headed for New York, presumably to the relief of
Augustus John if no one else; London's bohemians needed to look
to other places for their night-time entertainment. One of those
they chose was the Crabtree Club, founded by John himself in
premises above a shop in Greek Street, Soho. It was described by
the artist Paul Nash, who was clearly unimpressed, as, 'A place of
utter coarseness and dull unrelieved monotony'. Nash noted its
founder sitting there alone, 'a great pathetic muzzy god, a sort of
Silenus – but alas no nymphs, satyrs and leopards to complete
the picture'. However, it became a familiar late-night rendezvous
for artists, journalists, students and those younger members of
the upper classes who fancied dipping a toe in bohemian waters.
The glamorous model Betty May had happier memories of the

place than Nash. 'Everybody used to do *something* at the Crabtree,' she later wrote. 'They danced or played or were amusing in one way or another.' One of the club's regulars was the future novelist Jean Rhys, who described it as 'full of weedy youths drinking absinthe, trying hard to be vicious and hoping they looked French'. Nonetheless Rhys loved the place, frequently arriving after midnight and staying until six in the morning, and she was devastated when it closed.

Women in Bohemia

During the nineteenth century the entire female sex, with very few exceptions, was almost invisible in bohemia. It was an exclusively male preserve. Mistresses, models and prostitutes existed to service the assorted needs of bohemians, but they were kept in the background. The idea that a woman might herself be a bohemian and a creative artist was close to unthinkable. Changes began in the 1890s, but, even in the early decades of the twentieth century, women in bohemian London tended to be given only walk-on parts in the drama. They faced what Virginia Nicholson calls 'the hard-to-eradicate sexism of the bohemian male' – however free-spirited they were, women were still often expected to play handmaiden, muse or nursemaid to the male genius of the household. Even very gifted women painters in the Edwardian era, for example, were pushed out of sight. Gwen John was long overshadowed by her much more flamboyant brother Augustus and it is only in recent years that her work has been given its due. Dora Carrington's brilliance as an artist is now appreciated, but, for a long period after her death, interest in her focused not on her work but on her tangled relationships with Lytton Strachey and Ralph Partridge.

However, things were beginning to change. In 1914, the Café Royal was the scene of what was afterwards remembered as a

NANCY CUNARD, 1932, PHOTOGRAPHER UNKNOWN

pivotal moment in the history of women within bohemia. This
was the arrival there, unchaperoned, of two unconventional
products of the upper classes – Nancy Cunard and Iris Tree. Today
this seems hardly worthy of note, but, at the time, it was unusual,
indeed almost unprecedented. At the time, unattended women

in the Café Royal fell into the occasionally interchangeable categories of dancer, artists' model or prostitute. Yet here were two young women from impeccably respectable backgrounds staking their claim to a place within café society. Nancy Cunard was 18 in 1914 and impressed everyone who met her with her striking looks. 'She was very slim with a skin as white as bleached almonds, the bluest eyes one has ever seen and very fair hair,' wrote the novelist David Garnett. 'She was marvellous.' The great-granddaughter of the founder of the Cunard shipping line, she was born into great wealth, but rebelled against her privileged upbringing. In later years she was to be a poet, a muse to other writers and a tireless campaigner against racism and fascism. Her *Negro: An Anthology*, compiled after she embarked on a love affair with the African-American jazz musician Henry Crowder, remains a landmark volume in the history of black literature. Iris Tree, a year younger, was the daughter of the actor/manager Sir Herbert Beerbohm Tree. A friend of Cunard since schooldays, she attended the Slade School of Art, where she met and modelled for Dora Carrington. She also sat for other, older artists, including Augustus John, Vanessa Bell and Roger Fry, and secretly rented a flat in Fitzroy Place where she and Nancy could paint, write poetry and host late-night parties.

Tree and, particularly, Cunard had future roles to play in artistic and social life, but it was another woman, Nina Hamnett, who became known as the 'Queen of Bohemia'. Born in 1890 in Tenby, Pembrokeshire (also the home town of Augustus John), she studied art in London as a young woman and soon became a familiar face at the Café Royal and other bohemian haunts, renowned for her *joie de vivre* and love of a good party. She socialised with John and with other established artists like Walter Sickert and Jacob Epstein. She also met and modelled for a new generation of artists. Hamnett was particularly proud of her association with the sculptor Henri Gaudier-Brzeska and, in her drink-befuddled anecdotage in

PORTRAIT OF NINA HAMNETT, ROGER FRY, 1917

the pubs of Soho and Fitzrovia, she was in the habit of introducing herself with the enigmatic statement, 'You know me, m'dear. I'm in the V&A with me left tit knocked off'. Today she's actually in the Tate Collection, where Gaudier-Brzeska's 'Torso', for which she modelled, was transferred in 1983.

In 1914, she moved to Paris, where she danced naked on the tables of Montparnasse cafés and knew Modigliani, Picasso, Cocteau and many of the other lions of the city's avant-garde. Returning to London once the war began, she worked at the Omega Workshops under the auspices of Roger Fry, who painted a fine portrait of her which is currently in the Courtauld Gallery. (Hamnett's own talents as an artist have long been overlooked in favour of her reputation as a bohemian 'character', but she was herself a fine painter, particularly gifted as a portraitist.) During the 1920s, she became a fixture in the pubs of Soho and Fitzrovia, which were to be her stamping grounds for the rest of her life. In 1931, she published an autobiography, *Laughing Torso*, which is still in print and is still wonderfully, eccentrically readable. Three years later she was sued for libel by Aleister Crowley, who objected to what he claimed were her defamatory references to the black magic he had practised at his so-called Abbey of Thelema on the island of Sicily. Crowley lost his case, but the trial became a *cause célèbre*, covered with salacious glee by the popular press, and Nina found herself briefly a newspaper celebrity.

So too did her friend, the model Betty May, who appeared as a witness for the defence. May's career, and those of models like her, demonstrate how, even in the 1910s and 1920s, the easier route to attention for a woman in bohemia was to pose for paintings rather than create them. Born into a coster family in Canning Town in 1893, May grew up in poverty with few advantages in life other than her startling good looks. As we have seen, she took to frequenting the Café Royal as a young woman and it was there that she was talent-spotted by Jacob Epstein, who asked her to model for him. She rapidly became a fixture on the bohemian scene, famous for her dancing and her gypsy dress. She was known as the 'Tiger Woman', the title she gave to her 1929 autobiography. Differing stories exist to account for the nickname. Perhaps it was given to her during a visit to Paris where she had a catfight with a

BUST OF BETTY MAY BY JACOB EPSTEIN, 1920 OR EARLIER

rival for the affections of an Apache gangster. Perhaps it derived from a distinctive tiger-skin coat she regularly wore. Or from a party performance in which she would go down on all fours and lap brandy from a saucer. In court, during the Crowley libel case, she gave a more mundane reason for becoming a tiger woman. 'I am rather feline in looks,' she told the judge. 'I thought perhaps it was rather a good name for me.' May was invited to give evidence at the Hamnett libel trial because she had spent time at Crowley's Abbey with her husband Raoul Loveday, a young, Oxford-educated poet who had died there in 1923, allegedly as a consequence of drinking cat's blood in the course of a ritual sacrifice, and could vouch for what had gone on at Thelema.

In the wake of the Crowley trial both Hamnett and May contrived to take further financial advantage of their temporary notoriety. Sitting in the Fitzroy Tavern in Charlotte Street, Hamnett noticed a photograph in a newspaper that was captioned 'Miss Nina Hamnett takes a walk in the Park with a friend'. It was actually a photo of Betty May and an unidentified man. She rushed out of the pub, hailed a taxi and visited the newspaper offices, where she claimed to be so offended by the misidentification that she was thinking of suing the paper for libel. The paper gave her £25 to drop the idea and go away. Returning to the Fitzroy, she told the story to an audience which included Betty May. Shouting, 'I've been libelled too,' Betty immediately exited the pub and headed for Fleet Street. The newspaper forked out another £25 to keep her quiet as well.

Betty May was only the most famous of a troupe of other model muses who flit through the pages of memoirs of the period. There was Euphemia Lamb, who posed for Epstein and Augustus John and married the painter Henry Lamb, although marriage did little to restrict her adventurous sex life. John wrote in a letter that she had '6 men in her room last night, representing the six European powers' and Aleister Crowley, who was another of her lovers, described her in his autobiography as 'incomparably beautiful' and 'capable of stimulating the greatest extravagancies of passion'. There was Lilian Shelley, born in Bristol in 1892, who had been a music hall performer billed as 'The Merry, Mad, Magnetic Comedienne' before she became a model for Augustus John and the sculptor Jacob Epstein. A regular at both the Cave of the Golden Calf and John's Crabtree Club, where she danced and sang favourite numbers from her music hall years, such as the once-popular 'My Little Popsy-Wopsy', Shelley was described by Nina Hamnett as 'the craziest and most generous creature in the world'. Hamnett also claimed that one of Shelley's jobs at the Cave of the Golden Calf was to visit the Savoy Hotel at 10.30 every evening and feed the monkeys which Frida Strindberg kept in her room there. Shelley was still modelling for Epstein in the early 1920s, but disappeared from view in the years to come and died, probably a suicide, in the 1930s. (Epstein's models sometimes seem to have been fated to meet unfortunate ends. The Kashmiri Sunita Devi, whom the sculptor first encountered when she was selling trinkets at the British Empire Exhibition at Wembley in 1924, was killed – possibly murdered – when she returned to India in 1932.)

There was also Norine Schofield, more commonly known as 'Dolores', who modelled for Epstein and was described by him as 'a High Priestess of Beauty'. In 1929, her relationship with an artist named Frederick Atkinson attracted lurid newspaper attention after the 20-year old Atkinson gassed himself in his studio in Maida Vale. Dolores was portrayed in the cheap press as a vampish femme fatale who had toyed with the young painter's affections, and spent what little money he had, while simultaneously living with another man. She defended herself vigorously, claiming that she was a spiritualist and would soon be contacting Frederick to enlist his support in clearing her name, but almost immediately embarked on another ill-advised affair. This was with Philip Yale Drew, an alcoholic American actor whom the police strongly suspected of involvement in the murder of a tobacconist in Reading. The relationship between Drew and Dolores was one made in tabloid heaven and the papers had a field day, but it failed to last. Living in a variety of cheap rooms in Soho, Dolores was reduced to striking 'artistic poses' in a cheap funfair in Tottenham Court Road where another attraction was the Rector of Stiffkey, the Church of England vicar and self-styled 'Prostitutes' Padre', defrocked in 1932 for his over-enthusiastic commitment to rescuing young women from the dangers of the London streets. She was found dead in a Paddington basement in 1934, aged only 40.

The Seeds of Modernism and the Bloomsbury Group

In those years before the First World War, other bohemias could be found beyond the one inhabited by Augustus John and the artists of the Slade School. These varying artistic circles were not tightly defined and membership of one group did not preclude friendship or acquaintanceship with members of another. The decade before 1914 was the one in which the seeds of literary modernism were sown in London and many of the movement's pioneers were unmistakably bohemian in their habits and appearance. Ezra Pound and Wyndham Lewis in their younger years could both have posed for *Punch* illustrations of the average bohemian. Even TS Eliot who seemed in most respects the antithesis of the bohemian – the poet as bank clerk rather than rebel – had his unconventionalities which emerged in the years when he was tormented by the regular crises of his first marriage. He took to wearing face powder, faintly tinted green, and, Virginia Woolf noted in her diaries, 'I am not sure that he does not paint his lips'.

The American poet Ezra Pound arrived in London in the summer of 1908, moving into lodgings in Great Titchfield Street and throwing himself into the city's literary life with enormous élan. Both dandy and eccentric, he dressed in smartly coutured velvet jacket, Italian trousers and spats, but added to the effect by sporting a single turquoise earring, lapis lazuli blue buttons and an ebony black cane. Stories also began to circulate of Pound's sometimes outré behaviour. At a dinner given by Ernest Rhys, poet and founding editor of Everyman's Library, at his Hampstead house, he grew bored with fellow guest WB Yeats's lengthy discourse on poetry, and began to eat the floral centrepiece on the table, one tulip at a time. Afterwards, 'fortified if anything, by the tulips', in Rhys's words, he declaimed his 'Ballad of the Goodly Fere' with marked enthusiasm.

BOHEMIAN LONDON

EZRA POUND PHOTOGRAPHED BY ALVIN LANGDON COBURN,
OCTOBER 22, 1913

Pound's self-presentation as flamboyant bohemian could be more than matched by that of Wyndham Lewis. In his 1930s memoir *Return to Yesterday*, Ford Madox Ford includes an amusing description of his first meeting with Lewis on the stairs leading to the offices in Holland Park Avenue of Ford's magazine *The English Review*. 'He was extraordinary in appearance,' Ford writes, 'he seemed to be Russian. He was very dark in the shadows of the staircase. He wore an immense steeple-crowned hat. Long black locks fell from it. His coat was one of those Russian looking coats that have no revers. He had also an ample black cape of the type that villains in transpontine melodrama throw over their shoulders when they say, "Ha-ha!". He said not a word.' As Ford attempted to rid himself of this uninvited visitor, Lewis 'established himself immovably against the banisters and began fumbling in the pockets of his cape. He produced crumpled papers in rolls. He fumbled in the pockets of his strange coat. He produced crumpled papers in rolls. He produced them from all over his person – from inside his waistcoat, from against his skin beneath his brown jersey... All the time he said no word.'

The son of an English mother and an American father, Lewis was born in 1882 on a yacht off the coast of Nova Scotia, and lived in London after his parents separated in 1893. He studied at the Slade School of Art, where, as Ford's description of his appearance suggests, he was enormously impressed by Augustus John. In truth he had been overwhelmed by the older man. 'Near John,' he wrote in a letter, 'I can never paint, since his artistic personality is too great.' Lewis left the Slade without finishing his studies and lived for a time in Paris where he was exposed to Cubism and other cutting-edge movements in painting. Returning to London, he became a vociferous and quarrelsome figure in the capital's artistic avant-garde, prominent as painter, polemicist and writer.

Both Pound and Lewis were outsiders in London. At the same time that they were looking to impose themselves on its literary life, another strand of bohemianism was being nurtured in the heart of the city's cultural establishment. Sir Leslie Stephen was one of the great panjandrums of Victorian literature – a highly influential critic and essayist, and founding editor of the *Dictionary of National Biography*. In 1904, following Sir Leslie's death, his four children – Thoby, Adrian, Virginia and Vanessa – moved out of the family home in Hyde Park Gate and took a house in Gordon Square. Today, when Bloomsbury is largely a haunt of students and academics from the University of London, and tourists in search of the British Museum, it's hard to understand just what this meant. At the time Bloomsbury was simply not a place where upper middle-class young women could be expected to live. 'Beatrice comes round,' Virginia Stephen, later Woolf, wrote in a letter, referring to a worried friend, 'inarticulate with meaning, & begs me not to take the house because of the neighbourhood'.

The Stephens were soon the focus for a group which was not so much an organised movement in the arts, as it is sometimes wrongly portrayed, but more a collection of like-minded friends. Most of the men at the heart of 'Bloomsbury' had met one another at Trinity College, Cambridge, where Thoby Stephen, Lytton Strachey, Saxon Sydney-Turner, Clive Bell and Leonard Woolf had all studied. In vacations, visiting London, these young men had met up with Thoby Stephen's sisters Virginia and Vanessa and thus the embryonic Bloomsbury Group came into being. Once the young men had graduated and the Stephen siblings had moved to Gordon Square, they revelled in new-found freedoms and embarked on what would be, for some of them, long and productive careers in the arts. By some definitions of the word, it is difficult to categorise the Bloomsbury artists and intellectuals as 'bohemian'. If they were, they were upper middle-class bohemians who often found it difficult to forget that they were upper middle-class. They were bohemians who tended to employ maids and cooks to cater to their everyday needs.

However, there were two areas of life in which the Bloomsburyites were undoubted pioneers – art and sex. Leading Bloomsbury figures were instrumental in the introduction of Post-Impressionist art to British audiences. Painters such as Cézanne, Gauguin and Van Gogh were first shown in England at an exhibition in 1910 at the Grafton Galleries entitled 'Manet and the Post-Impressionists'. Organised by the artist and critic Roger Fry, it proved a revelation to Bloomsbury painters like Vanessa Bell and Duncan Grant, although other visitors were roused to fury and mockery by many of the works on display. One critic described some of the paintings as 'the work of madmen' and another was of the opinion that the exhibition could only be of interest to 'students of pathology and the specialist in abnormality'. Its notoriety was only increased by a 'Post-Impressionist Ball', at which Virginia and Vanessa Stephen turned up as 'Gauguin girls', half-dressed in brightly coloured fabrics. 'We wore brilliant fabrics and beads,' Vanessa later remembered, 'we browned our legs and arms, and had very little on beneath the draperies.' The society in which the Stephen sisters had grown up was scandalised.

It would have been even more scandalised had it known of the growing freedom within Bloomsbury circles to speak about anything – particularly the freedom for both sexes to talk about sex. In a well-known passage of autobiographical writing, Virginia Woolf recalled one spring evening in Gordon Square in the late Edwardian years when she and Vanessa were visited by 'the long and sinister figure of Mr Lytton Strachey'.

'He pointed his finger at a stain on Vanessa's white dress. "Semen?" he said… With that one word all barriers of reticence and reserve went down. A flood of the sacred fluid seemed to overwhelm us. Sex permeated our conversation. The word bugger was never far from our lips. We discussed copulation with the same excitement and openness that we had discussed the nature of goodness.' Although the scene may not have occurred precisely as Woolf remembered it – 'I do not know if I invented it or not', she confessed – it was an important moment in the history of the Bloomsbury Group.

The Bloomsburyites did not restrict themselves to just talking about sex. They have famously been described as people who lived in squares and loved in triangles. Vanessa Stephen married the art critic Clive Bell, but had affairs with the artist and critic Roger Fry and the painter Duncan Grant. The bisexual Grant had numerous relationships with men, including the economist John Maynard Keynes, the novelist David Garnett and Lytton Strachey, who was long besotted with him. Strachey was adored by Dora Carrington, but she married Ralph Partridge, who was, in turn, the object of Strachey's admiration. Vanessa's daughter Angelica believed her father to be Clive Bell, but was told when she was 18 that she was actually fathered by Duncan Grant. Six years later she married David Garnett, who had been her true father's lover more than 20 years earlier. Just reading about the tangled webs of Bloomsbury relationships can be confusing. How much more so it must have been to have lived through them.

As has been noted above, the various bohemias of Edwardian London were not self-contained cliques. They regularly interacted with one another. One of the places where Bloomsbury intellectuals and Slade School artists met and mingled was the Omega Workshops, which were established at 33 Fitzroy Square in July 1913. These were the brainchild of Roger Fry. Fry's fellow directors were Duncan Grant and Vanessa Bell and other artists connected to the workshops during their six years of existence included the Jewish East End painter Mark Gertler, Edward Wadsworth, David Bomberg and William Roberts. So significant a place do the Omega Workshops hold in the history of early twentieth-century British art and design that it's difficult to believe that many of its products may not have been much good. Yet, if Wyndham Lewis is to be credited, 'the chairs we sold stuck to the seats of people's trousers; when they took up an Omega candlestick, they couldn't put it down again, they held it in an involuntary vice-like grip. It was glued to them and they to it.' Lewis, a belligerent man at the best of times and one who fell out with Roger Fry soon after the opening of the Workshops, may not be a disinterested critic, but it does seem likely that some of the available goods did not meet the high standards that the Omega's founder would have hoped to attain. A more sympathetic witness, Naomi Mitchison, also claimed that the lamps she purchased there were shoddily constructed and that the lampshades that went with them were made of such thin silk that they quickly rotted.

KATE LECHMERE, REBEL ART CENTRE, 1914, PHOTOGRAPHER UNKNOWN

In March 1914, Lewis was the driving force behind the establishment of the Rebel Art Centre in Great Ormond Street. In some ways Lewis intended it as a direct rival to the Omega Workshops, but it was even shorter lived. It lasted only a few months, closing in the summer of the year it opened, although, as the birthplace of Vorticism, often described as the only major modernist art movement to be created solely in England, and of *Blast*, Lewis's polemical magazine, it had an influence beyond its brief existence. Other artists involved in the Rebel Art Centre, most of them, like Lewis, disgruntled refugees from the Omega, included Christopher Nevinson, Edward Wadsworth, Frederick Etchells and Spencer Gore. Many of them pitched in to create the Centre's Vorticist decorations, although these were not to everybody's taste. According to Violet Hunt, novelist and lover of Ford Madox Ford, the murals made the place look like 'a butcher's shop full of prime cuts... the blood running down in gouts and streaks on the cornices and folding doors'. The money for the Rebel Art Centre came from the painter Kate Lechmere, then romantically involved with Lewis. Lechmere later transferred her affections to the Imagist poet and critic TE Hulme – the resulting triangle was at the heart of one of the most mythologised scuffles in the history of English modernism when Lewis stormed through Soho in search of Hulme, with Lechmere at his heels pleading, 'Please don't kill him, please don't.' In the end it was Hulme, much the more muscular of the two men, who got the better of Lewis and hung him upside down on the railings of Soho Square.

One of the few shows put on at the Rebel Art Centre during its brief existence was an exhibition of sculptures by Henri Gaudier-Brzeska. Henri Gaudier was a Frenchman, born near Orléans in 1891, who came to London to work as an artist when he was 19. Accompanying him was a would-be writer from Poland called Sophie Brzeska, 18 years his senior. They lived together and he took her name, although they never married and the exact nature of their undoubtedly intense relationship remains unclear. (It seems unlikely that they had sex more than once or twice, and Sophie preferred, when in funds, to buy Henri the services of prostitutes.) Gaudier-Brzeska is reported by Nina Hamnett to have said that, 'Artists should be poor and not indulge in comforts of any kind'. He certainly lived by this precept himself. He was so poor that he couldn't afford to go into even the most modest of Soho restaurants – which he tended to damn as too 'bourgeois' anyway – and was once seen squatting on the corner of Old Compton Street and Dean Street, tucking into a crust of bread and a lump of cheese. Gaudier-Brzeska was also, according to Richard Aldington, 'probably the dirtiest human being I have ever known' and 'gave off horrid effluvia in hot weather', sufficient to drive Ford Madox Ford from the room when he was once obliged to sit next to the sculptor. Whatever his shortcomings in personal hygiene, Gaudier-Brzeska was a brilliant and innovative sculptor whose gifts, as the Rebel Art Centre exhibition shows, were just beginning to be recognised when the First World War began. He enlisted in the French army almost immediately and was killed in the trenches in June 1915. Sophie, to whom he bequeathed most of his artworks, died in a mental hospital in Gloucestershire ten years later.

The First World War struck at bohemia as it did every other level of society. Gaudier-Brzeska was not the only bohemian to lose his life in the conflict – TE Hulme, the man who had hung Wyndham Lewis upside down on the railings of Soho Square, was killed by a shell while serving as an artillery officer in Flanders. And, on the home front, bohemian life was intensified by the war. 'It sometimes seemed,' Betty May later wrote, 'as if everyone one had ever known would be killed – one went on dancing and rioting in an effort to forget how dreadful it all was.' Augustus John's parties at his house and studio in Mallord Street, Chelsea became notorious, although some descriptions can make them sound fairly staid affairs. Carrington writes of one she attended in a letter of July 1917 to Lytton Strachey. 'It had been given in honour of a favourite barmaid of the pub in Chelsea, near Mallord Street, as she was leaving. She looked a charming character, very solid, with bosoms, and a fat pouting face. It was great fun. Joseph, a splendid man from one of those cafés in Fitzroy Street, played a concertina, and another man a mandolin. John as drunk as a King Fisher. Many dreadfully worn characters, moth eaten and decrepit who I gathered were artists of Chelsea.' John, she reports, 'made many serious attempts to wrest my virginity from me. But he was too mangy to tempt me even for a second'.

As the war went on, the use of sex, drink and drugs as means of escape from its realities increased. Cocaine, hitherto largely confined to the pages of Sherlock Holmes stories and to a small band of initiates, became a drug of choice, particularly amongst the inhabitants of the theatrical world, where boundaries between the respectable and the unrespectable were rarely defined with any clarity. Lurid stories of dope girls and dope fiends began to appear in the press. One newspaper gossip columnist, 'Quex' of the *Evening News*, wrote of the prevalence of 'that exciting drug cocaine' in what he termed 'West End bohemia'.

'It is so easy to take,' he went on, 'just snuffed up the nose; and no-one seems to know why the girls who suffer from this body- and soul-racking habit find the drug so easy to obtain.' One of the reasons may have been that dozens and dozens of varyingly dodgy nightclubs existed in which drugs of all kinds were offered for sale. In a misguided attempt to regulate London nightlife during the war, the authorities imposed a curfew on clubs in 1915. The unanticipated consequence was that the clubs were driven underground. By the end of the year there were, reportedly, 150 illegal nightclubs just in Soho and many of them were awash with drugs, particularly the newly popular cocaine.

Inevitably there were casualties of this expansion in the availability of drugs. Probably the most notorious of these was the actress Billie Carleton, who died of a cocaine overdose in November 1918 in her suite at the Savoy Hotel less than three weeks after the end of the war. Carleton, a former chorus girl for the impresario CB Cochran, had graduated to larger roles in musical comedies and, at the time of her death, was starring in a show called *The Freedom of the Seas* at the Haymarket Theatre. After attending a Victory Ball at the Royal Albert Hall, dressed in a notably revealing costume, she was found dead in her bed by her maid. Tabloid newspapers went to town on the Carleton case and others with eye-catching headlines about dope parties and orgies. The *Daily Express* had a report from a special correspondent, who risked who knew what by attending a gathering in a Piccadilly flat where there were 'sensual-coloured carpets… low-shaded purple lights and an uncanny atmosphere of lassitude' and the host 'lisped like a woman, had a nervous, jerky motion of the hands and reeked overpoweringly of perfume'.

Chapter Five

BOHEMIA IN THE TWENTIES AND THIRTIES

The Bright Young Things

WILD SOCIALISING during the war allowed people to forget the fighting. When the war came to an end, the dissipation did not. In Twenties London, the urge to party until one dropped seemed to grow even stronger. For some, it could all become too much. There is no mistaking the weary disdain expressed by Evelyn Waugh at the end of the decade in the now famous paragraph from his novel *Vile Bodies* – 'Masked parties, Savage parties, Victorian parties, Greek parties, Wild West parties, Russian parties, Circus parties, parties where one had to dress as somebody else, almost naked parties in St John's Wood, parties in flats and studios and houses and ships and hotels and nightclubs, in windmills and swimming-baths, tea parties at school where one drank brown sherry and smoked Turkish cigarettes, dull dances in London and comic dances in Scotland and disgusting dances in Paris – all that succession and repetition of massed humanity... Those vile bodies.'

REX WHISTLER PHOTOGRAPHED BY HOWARD COSTER, 1936

Yet it was also Waugh, looking back on his youth from late middle age, who wrote, 'There was between the wars a society, cosmopolitan, sympathetic to the arts, well-mannered, above all ornamental even in rather bizarre ways, which for want of a better description, the newspapers called "High Bohemia".' This was the same milieu that DJ Taylor described as 'a new kind of "smart bohemia", open both to an avant-garde artist and a baronet's daughter' and it centred on the disparate group of individuals dubbed 'The Bright Young Things' by the press. The Bright Young Things ranged from the rich and frivolous to genuinely talented artists. Lytton Strachey's supposed dismissal of a group he met at Wilsford Manor, Stephen Tennant's home in Wiltshire, as 'strange creatures with just a few feathers where brains should be' was not entirely fair. Whatever else one might say about Evelyn Waugh, Cecil Beaton, Rex Whistler, Robert Byron and Nancy Mitford (all of whom could be classified as, or were strongly associated with, the 'Bright Young Things'), it's impossible to deny that they were both intelligent and gifted.

Who then were the Bright Young Things? Throughout the 1920s, a 'haut bohemia' circled around the likes of Lady Diana Manners and Nancy Cunard, the woman who had made such an impression as a teenager by daring to visit the Café Royal unchaperoned. However, both Manners and Cunard were born in the 1890s and were contemporaries of men who fought in the First World War. Indeed Manners, later Lady Diana Cooper, had worked as a nurse during the conflict and both women had lost men they loved. The Bright Young Things came from a slightly later generation. Very nearly all of them were born in the first decade of the twentieth century and were children or adolescents during the war. Some, like Stephen Tennant and Henry Thynne, were from an aristocratic background; others, like Waugh and Whistler, were scions of the professional middle classes, determined to parlay their artistic talents into social success.

Their activities soon attracted the attentions of the press. Several of the Bright Young Things themselves worked as journalists and they were not slow to publicise the adventures of their friends. The parties continued through the decade. The actress Tallulah Bankhead entertained guests in her flat in Farm

Street, Mayfair and was known to open the door to new arrivals in the nude before leading them off for cocktails. Norman Hartnell, a couturier later known for the dresses he designed for the royal family, held a circus-themed party in Bruton Street in July 1929. Acrobats, performing bears and Siberian wolf cubs mingled with the guests, while Lady Eleanor Smith, daughter of a Tory peer, led a white pony up the main staircase and Bright Young Things danced to a jazz band and a circus orchestra. Babies provided the theme for another party that July. Guests headed towards the Rutland Gate home of socialite Rosemary Sandars dressed as giant infants and downed drinks in baby bottles. One of the parties best remembered in future years was the poet and socialite Brian Howard's 'Great Urban Dionysia', which was held in Marylebone Lane a few months earlier. Those invited were told to arrive dressed as characters from Greek mythology. Around its border the 16-inch-high invitation listed those things Howard adored (Picasso, Nietzsche, Jazz, the Mediterranean and so on), and those he abhorred (Public Schools, Debutantes, Sadist Devotees of Blood-sports, Hilaire Belloc). It was a brief catalogue of his generation's tastes.

One of the delights of London life that the Bright Young Things very definitely adored rather than abhorred was a good nightclub. Probably the best known of the 1920s night spots was The 43 Club in Gerrard Street, owned and run by Kate Meyrick, an Irishwoman in her fifties. Its reputation was enhanced both by the fame and social standing of some of its clientele and by its proprietor's regular appearances in the law courts. A prosecuting lawyer had once described an earlier club run by Mrs Meyrick as 'a noxious fungus growth upon our social system' and the 43 proved similarly controversial. Visitors may have ranged from King Carol of Romania to Rudolph Valentino, but Mrs Meyrick was arrested several times for breaking licensing laws. Her ultimate downfall came in 1928 when she was prosecuted for bribing a police officer. Sergeant George Goddard, who had led an earlier police raid on

KATE MEYRICK, PROPRIETOR OF THE 43 CLUB AT 43 GERRARD STREET, 1930

the 43, was found to have the then substantial sum of £12,000 hidden at home, much of it built up by taking £100 a week from Mrs Meyrick as protection money. In the last analysis, since three of her daughters married into the aristocracy, Mrs Meyrick may well have felt that her venture was a resounding success. The 43 Club and its proprietor appear, thinly disguised as the Old Hundredth and 'Ma' Mayfield, in Evelyn Waugh's novel *Brideshead Revisited*. (Waugh also immortalised another social haunt of the Bright Young Things and its eccentric owner. The Cavendish Hotel in Jermyn Street was run by Rosa Lewis, reputedly once a mistress of Edward VII. In Waugh's novel *Vile Bodies* she is transformed into Lottie Crump and her establishment into Shepheard's Hotel.)

The Cave of Harmony in Gower Street was opened in 1924 by Elsa Lanchester, in later life the wife of Charles Laughton and star of the Hollywood film *Bride of Frankenstein*, but at that time a cabaret artiste whose speciality was performing Victorian ballads with altered and risqué lyrics. The Cave was soon a haunt of the louche and, often, the gay. The painter Robert Medley, in his later autobiography, remembered his nights there with great affection. 'I was a good dancer and I decided to show off with Elsa in a tango,' he wrote of one occasion. 'She suddenly announced in her clear voice, "The trouble with you, Robert, is that you don't know what sex you are!" As everybody had been looking on, the only reply to this deadly shaft was to take off all my clothes and demonstrate the facts. This unpremeditated exhibition was greeted with a round of applause. It was evidently what was needed to get the party going and I was not allowed to get dressed again.'

The Gargoyle Club was founded in 1925 at 69 Dean Street and run by the rich socialite David Tennant, brother of Stephen, as a refuge for the artistically avant-garde and those members of the aristocracy and the wealthy elite who had a taste for the unconventional. 'Above all,' Tennant proclaimed, 'it will be a place without the usual rules where people can express themselves freely.' Over the years those who came to the Gargoyle to express themselves freely included nearly all of the most recognisable names in London's bohemia, from Nancy Cunard and Brian Howard to Dylan Thomas and Augustus John. Henri Matisse was a friend of the Gargoyle's founder and not only did several of the French painter's works hang in the club, but its glass ballroom had been designed by Tennant in consultation with him. It was on the upper floors of the building and access to it was via 'a coffin large enough for two, which was called the lift'. The club even ran to a rooftop garden where drinking and dancing under the moonlight were possible on summer evenings.

The Harlequin, a club and restaurant, was in Beak Street. This was the scene of the wedding of the argumentative South African poet Roy Campbell and Mary, one of the famously beautiful Garman sisters. According to Campbell, 'No other contemporary

ROY & MARY CAMPBELL (LEFT), JACOB KRAMER & DOLORES, 1920s

women ever had so much poetry, good, bad and indifferent, written about them, or had so many portraits and busts made of them'. He had met Mary by chance and moved into the flat she shared with her younger sister Kathleen in Regent Square. There, fuelled largely by beer and the radishes he ate, leaves and all, in great numbers, Campbell set about writing the poetry that he hoped would make him famous. He and Mary went through a 'gypsy' marriage ceremony, conducted by a friend of Augustus John, but they decided that a more conventional wedding in the bride's home town in Staffordshire was also required. Having shocked the more shockable members of the extended Garman family by turning up at the altar in shoes with holes in them plugged by newspaper, Campbell took his new wife back to London and the Harlequin. There, booze in large quantities was available for the guests. The party continued after the newly-weds had retired to bed and, in the words of Augustus John, 'the guests then became quarrelsome'. He and fellow artist Jakob Kramer began a noisy argument over the respective sizes of their biceps, which threatened to end in violence until Campbell, disturbed from his nuptial bed, came back into the room and said he would throw Kramer out of the window if he didn't shut up. Impressed by Campbell's height and air of menace, Kramer shut up.

It was also at the Harlequin that Kathleen Garman was approached by a middle-aged man with wild hair and intense eyes who turned out to be the sculptor Jacob Epstein. He asked her to sit for him and she rapidly became his mistress. Epstein's wife Margaret had always been tolerant of her husband's many infidelities, and she was even bringing up his daughter by a previous model, the actress Meum Stewart, but she disliked Kathleen, recognising her as a genuine rival for Epstein's attentions and affections. In the summer of 1923, Margaret invited Kathleen to her house while Epstein was away and shot her in the shoulder with a pearl-handled pistol. Kathleen recovered in hospital and the incident was hushed up. She continued her relationship with Epstein and they had three children together: Theodore, an artist who suffered from schizophrenia and died before his thirtieth birthday; Esther, who committed suicide six months after her brother's death; and Kitty, who became the first wife of Lucian Freud and appears in many of his early paintings. Epstein and Kathleen eventually married, after Margaret's death, in 1955.

Despite their connection through the Garmans, Epstein and Campbell did not get on. When the poet was living in Regent Square, sharing the flat with both sisters, a jealous Epstein had been convinced (incorrectly) that Campbell was sleeping with both Mary and Kathleen. On one occasion, he turned up at the flat in a fury to treat the sisters to a tirade against Campbell and his lack of morals. Unbeknown to him, the poet was actually in the flat at the time, hiding behind the piano, and, as Epstein continued to rant and rave, Campbell kept the women amused by popping up from his hiding place and making silly faces. After his marriage, when he was still living in a flat above the Harlequin,

JACOB EPSTEIN AND HIS WIFE KATHLEEN GARMAN, 1953

Campbell even got into a fight with the much older Epstein. 'A chest of drawers fell over,' Campbell later wrote. 'I sat quietly on his stomach as he lay philosophically blinking at the ceiling and quite conscious… I went out to find Augustus John and Mary, having sustained nothing more than a scratch on the forehead from Epstein's waist-coat buttons as I threw him over my head.'

The Harlequin was owned by Johnny Papani, a former waiter at the Café Royal. Ambitious to expand, Johnny later removed walls in the basement to make the restaurant larger. Following a series of offences against the licensing laws, he was jailed briefly, but proved a model prisoner. He was released early and made his way back home, delighted to be there sooner than he expected. As the unlucky Johnny opened the door to the Harlequin, the whole house collapsed over his head and killed him. The basement walls he had removed had been essential supports to the building.

Other clubs flourished, sometimes briefly, and then passed into history, to be replaced by still more. There was the Blue Lantern in Ham Yard. Dalton Murray ran the Morgue, also in Ham Yard, where the receptionist dressed as a nun, the waiters as devils and coffins were used as tables. There was the Hell Club in Gerrard Street, which, according to the memory of one patron, 'had hidden lighting that changed colour slowly, at a time when this was quite a novelty, and sank from pink to deep red and into ghastly purple and with various effects to make flickering shadows'. Also in Gerrard Street was the Big Apple, which, unusually for the time, was a club that catered particularly for a black clientele. Some of these 1920s clubs were much more openly and obviously disreputable than the 43. At the Falstaff in Oxford Street, according to one man who had worked there, 'All the thieves and prostitutes of London came... to spend their money, and they demanded licence. Women for ten shillings a bet walked naked through the rooms. Men walked openly from group to group vending stolen articles. And on the dancefloor men lifted the skirts of girls as they passed and smacked their bare buttocks.' The club was eventually closed by the police after a succession of razor fights broke out involving the infamous Sabini gang.

Amidst all the press stories of the Bright Young Things, older ideas of bohemia still persisted in the popular imagination. A *Punch* cartoon of 1930 shows a troop of scruffy, bearded and eccentrically dressed men and short-haired women with cigarettes in holders being shepherded through a London street by a handful of bow-tied waiters. The caption reads: 'A herd of wild bohemians being rounded up for the opening of a new café in Soho, with the idea of creating the right atmosphere.' It could have appeared in the pages of the magazine at almost any time in the previous three decades. Indeed, alongside the new generation, a longer established bohemia, focused on artists like Augustus John and Jacob Epstein, continued to thrive. The Café Royal still opened its doors to a wide-ranging and often eccentric clientele, but, by the 1920s, it had been in existence for 60 years. It had also been recently refurbished and largely rebuilt in a way that had failed to please many of its old regulars. 'They might as well have told us,' TWH Crosland later wrote, 'that the British Empire was to be pulled down and redecorated.'

If one place could be said to embody 1920s bohemia in all its incarnations, it would probably be the Eiffel Tower restaurant in Percy Street. Nancy Cunard even wrote a poem to it (not a very good one, it has to be said) and claimed that, 'I think the Tower shall go up to heaven/One night in a flame of fire, about eleven,' 'If ever we go to heaven in a troop,' she continued, 'the Tower must be our ladder.' The restaurant was run by Rudolf Stulik, a plump, moustachioed Viennese who was reputed to have once been chef to the Austrian Emperor Franz Josef. It had long been a haunt of poets and painters. Ezra Pound, TE Hulme and the Poets' Club had met there in 1909 and the Tate today holds a well-known work by William Roberts entitled 'The Vorticists at the Restaurant de la Tour Eiffel, Spring 1915', painted in the early sixties, which nostalgically recalls a gathering during the First World War. Wyndham Lewis, at one time a neighbour of Stulik's in Percy Street, decorated a room in the restaurant in the Vorticist style. However, its heyday as a bohemian rendezvous was the twenties, when everybody who was or became anybody used it. Inevitably, Augustus John was a regular visitor, once dining there on peacocks before embarking on a visit to the USA. Other patrons included Walter Sickert, Tallulah Bankhead and the ubiquitous Nina Hamnett. Stulik built up a significant collection of modern art due to his habit of taking payment in drawings and paintings from impoverished artists, but he also played host to a wealthy and aristocratic clientele which enjoyed the idea of brief excursions into bohemia. The popularity of his restaurant continued into the following decade. On one famous occasion in 1936, the Austrian presented Augustus John with a bill for £43. 'I know you cheat me outrageously, Stulik,' John remarked, 'but £43 for lunch for two seems a bit steep.' 'Is not for lunch,' the restaurateur replied. 'Little Welshman with curly hair. He stay two weeks and eat. He say you pay.' Dylan Thomas was already launched on his lifelong career as a bohemian sponger and freeloader.

Court Cases and Casualties

In retrospect, the era of the Bright Young Things has been impossibly glamorised, its parties, excesses and extravagances celebrated in dozens of books, films and TV dramas. Beneath the hedonism, there was a dark side to 1920s bohemianism. It can be glimpsed in the fate of Freda Kempton. Freda was a 'dancing instructress' at the 43 Club, who took cocaine as a means of keeping awake during her long hours of work. The Chinese drug dealer, Brilliant Chang, whose name had been mentioned in the Billie Carleton case four years earlier, was reported to have supplied her with the drug on the night of 5 March 1922. The following day, Freda emerged from the bedroom of her flat in Westbourne Grove complaining of an excruciating headache. The pain got worse until she was banging her head against the wall because of it and then she began to convulse and foam at the mouth. She died in the arms of her landlady. At the inquest, Chang was closely questioned, but there was insufficient evidence to charge him with manslaughter and the jury finally reached the improbable verdict that Freda had committed suicide whilst temporarily insane. Chang was deported four years later after serving a prison sentence for supplying an actress named Violet Payne with cocaine.

Meanwhile, as Robert Medley danced the night away at the Cave of Harmony, other less lucky gay men faced prosecution. In the early hours of 16 January 1927, police officers arrived at a flat in Fitzroy Square to arrest those present. Pushing past the woman who answered the door, they confronted a man clad in 'a thin black transparent skirt, with gilt trimming round the edge and a red sash'. He was also, according to a later police report, wearing 'ladies shoes and was naked from the loins upwards'. His name was Bobby Britt. He was a dancer in the chorus of the West End hit *Lady Be Good*, starring Fred and Adele Astaire, and he was, he said, about to perform a 'Salome' dance for some friends. The police were unimpressed. They had been spying on Britt's flat for weeks and they hadn't much liked what they'd seen. Police Sergeant Arthur Spencer had seen two men leave who were undoubtedly 'of the Nancy type'. He had followed them and, he reported, 'They walked cuddling one another to Tottenham Court Road, where they stood waiting for a bus. I stood close to them and saw their faces were powdered and painted and their appearance and manner strongly suggested them to be importuners of men.' In the court case that followed, poor Bobby Britt was found guilty of keeping a disorderly house and sentenced to 15 months' hard labour. It's good to be able to report that he not only survived the experience, but went on to a long career as a dancer in the West End and on Broadway, and died, a centenarian, in 2000.

As the Carleton and Kempton cases and others indicated, there were plenty of casualties in the war against social convention. Several of the Bright Young Things were later to fall by the wayside, wounded and (in some instances) killed by their dependence on alcohol and drugs. Brian Howard never fulfilled the promise he showed as a young man and is doomed to be remembered as one of the inspirations for the sublimely camp Anthony Blanche in Evelyn Waugh's *Brideshead Revisited*, rather than as the great poet he wanted to be. In 1958, plagued by ill-health and broken-hearted by the accidental death of a lover, Howard took an overdose of sedatives and died himself, listening to 'Liebestod' from Wagner's *Tristan und Isolde*. The only biography of him that has been published is (uncompromisingly, if rather bleakly) entitled *Portrait of a Failure*.

BRENDA DEAN PAUL, 1952

Brenda Dean Paul, the daughter of a baronet and a Belgian pianist, was one of the great society beauties of her generation, but fell victim to the cocaine and heroin that were freely available at the more exotic parties of the 1920s. She became notorious in the tabloid press for her court appearances and spent most of the 1930s in and out of either nursing homes or Holloway Prison, relentlessly pursued by the authorities as a 'celebrity' addict. By the 1950s, she had returned to an earlier career on the stage, appearing in a production of the Ronald Firbank play *The Princess Zoubaroff*, but she was still attracting the attention of the police. As one person who saw her, the actor Neville Phillips, noted, the presence in the leading role of a 'once ravishing, now ravaged... society blonde lesbian drug addict' added to the audience's interest, as they enjoyed the 'extra frisson of wondering if the police might burst in at any moment and make an on-stage arrest'. Brenda Dean Paul died in 1959, worn out and still addicted, at the age of 52.

The 1930s and English Surrealism

The 1930s saw a distinct change in the nature of bohemian venues. Cafés, nightclubs and restaurants became less important. In the course of the decade, it was pubs that became central to London bohemia – most significantly, the pubs in the area that hadn't yet attracted the name of Fitzrovia. (The name reportedly first appeared in print in a newspaper article by Tom Driberg in 1940, although it may well have been used in everyday speech earlier than that.) The Fitzroy Tavern was – and still is – in Charlotte Street. Originally built as a coffee house in the 1880s, it was soon converted into a pub, but it was only after a Polish immigrant to London called Judah Kleinfeld took over the licence in 1919 that it gradually became one of the best-known watering-holes in the area. The pub's fame spread even further in the 1930s after 'Pop' Kleinfeld retired and handed over the licence to his daughter Annie and her husband Charlie Allchild. The bohemian invasion of the Fitzroy had begun in the previous decade when Augustus John and Nina Hamnett both took to drinking there and became friends with the Kleinfeld family. Within a short time it was the resort of artists and writers who needed an escape from their easels and their typewriters.

In the Fitzroy they could mix with such eccentric regulars as Prince Monolulu, the racing tipster who claimed to be African royalty. (He was actually called Peter McKay and came from the Danish West Indies. Monolulu was renowned at racecourses around the country for his flamboyant, idiosyncratic dress sense and for his cry of, 'I gotta horse! I gotta horse!' He was sufficiently well known in his day to appear as himself in half a dozen films and a pub in Maple Street, Fitzrovia was once named after him.) They could buy drinks for colleagues from less culturally reputable fields. Because they receive the most attention, it is easy to assume that all the Soho and Fitzrovian bohemians of the first half of the twentieth century were purveyors of high art – poets, painters and writers of literary fiction. In fact, there were pulp-fiction bohemians as well. Gwyn Evans, a regular in the Fitzroy, led a life of exemplary disorderliness and drunkenness, as archetypally self-destructive as his fellow Welshman Dylan Thomas. He even died young in 1938, aged 39, the same age as Thomas was when he died in America 15 years later. Evans, however, mostly wrote not poetry, but stories about Sexton Blake, the poor man's Sherlock Holmes.

Neither Sherlock Homes nor Sexton Blake was needed to throw light on the sad tale of one 1930s murder involving some of the Fitzroy Tavern's regular patrons. In 1936, the writer and occultist Douglas Bose was living with Sylvia Gough, who was twice his age and a former heiress, Ziegfeld Follies dancer and model for Augustus John. Bose was treating her badly. Aroused to ill-judged chivalry by the sight of Gough arriving in the pub with a black eye, Douglas Burton, a book reviewer and habitué of the Fitzroy, later struck Bose with a sculptor's hammer during a party at a flat in Canonbury and killed him. At his trial, Burton claimed that he had been driven mad by his unrequited infatuation with 'Tiger Woman' Betty May and that he had committed murder in a state of temporary insanity. His defence was a success and he was sent to a mental asylum rather than the gallows. Sylvia Gough continued to frequent the Fitzroy throughout the forties and fifties, sitting by the fire and becoming an increasingly frail and tattered memorial to its past history.

The 1930s was the decade in which surrealism first gained a tentative foothold on English soil. Thoroughly French in its origins, the movement in the arts had emerged in 1920s Paris (André Breton's first *Surrealist Manifesto* had been published in 1924), but its influence had now crossed the Channel and been felt by a number of British artists. John Banting, a painter and friend of both Brian Howard and Nancy Cunard, took to dyeing his hair green and wearing shoes with the tops cut off to display his painted toenails. Banting had previously been involved in the greatest art hoax of the 1920s. On 23 July 1929, an exhibition of paintings by Bruno Hat opened in the London home of Bryan Guinness, then the husband of Diana Mitford. The paintings were said to have been discovered in a remote French village, where they were hanging on the walls of a shop owned by Hat's mother. The artist made an appearance at the exhibition, wearing dark glasses, sitting in a wheelchair and speaking in a foreign accent. The newspapers hailed a new genius of modern art. In fact, Bruno Hat did not exist. He was the invention of Brian Howard. The paintings had been created by Howard and Banting as a prank and the man in the wheelchair was Guinness's brother-in-law, Tom Mitford, in heavy disguise. The pranksters owned up to their trickery soon after the exhibition's opening night.

The high point of English surrealism was undoubtedly the International Surrealist Exhibition which took place at the New Burlington Galleries in 1936. Organised largely by the artist and critic Roland Penrose and the youthful poet David Gascoyne, its intention was to introduce British audiences to the surrealist work being done in Paris and thus free them from what Penrose called 'the constipation of logic'. Some of the Parisian surrealists actually turned up for the exhibition's opening night on 11 June. Salvador Dali arrived in a diving suit, probably intended to symbolise his attempts to plumb the depths of the subconscious in his work, but it soon became clear that he was having great difficulty breathing inside it. After a number of fruitless attempts to break the glass on the helmet with a hammer, which succeeded only in adding ringing ears to Dali's other discomforts, a man with a spanner managed to wrench the helmet off the unfortunate artist. André Breton, the so-called 'Pope of Surrealism', put in an appearance with his wife, who, like some earlier incarnation of Lady Gaga, was wearing a piece of steak on her shoulder. Blood was running down her back to a notice which read, 'EAT ME'. Home-grown talents were also in evidence. Dylan Thomas attended and was seen approaching fellow guests with a cup full of boiled string and asking in a loud voice whether they wanted it weak or strong. The enigmatic Sheila Legge, whose biographical details remain elusive, was photographed in Trafalgar Square with her head hidden by a giant bunch of roses. She later appeared at the exhibition, making her way through the crowd with an artificial leg in one hand and a rapidly mouldering pork chop in the other.

Despite the best efforts of Penrose and Gascoyne and the *succès de scandale* of the International Surrealist Exhibition, surrealism never properly took off in Britain, although sporadic meetings of the London Surrealist Group continued after the war in the Barcelona Restaurant in Beak Street, Soho and the Horseshoe pub on Tottenham Court Road. One of the participants in the Monday night gatherings at the Barcelona was the young George Melly, who once read out a poem he had written which included the line, 'You are advised to take with you an umbrella in case it should rain knives and forks'. As an illustration of his odd image he hurled into the air a small collection of cutlery he had filched from the restaurant's sideboard. The resulting clatter was met with great applause by the assembled Surrealists, but annoyed the proprietor of the Barcelona so much that they were all thrown out into the street.

Chapter Six

FITZROVIA IN THE FORTIES

'Only beware of Fitzrovia,' Tambi said... It's a dangerous place, you must be careful.'

'Fights with knives?'

'No, a worse danger. You might get Sohoitis, you know.'

'No, I don't. What is it?'

'If you get Sohoitis,' Tambi said very seriously, 'you will stay there always day and night and get no work done ever.'

JULIAN MACLAREN-ROSS, *Memoirs of the Forties*

Fitzrovia Before It Was Fitzrovia

IN THE 1940s, no part of London, not even Soho, was as closely associated with bohemianism as Fitzrovia. The area around Fitzroy Street and Charlotte Street had long been home to artists and writers. One of the country's most famous painters, John Constable, had a house and studio at 76 Charlotte Street and died there in 1837. He was not the first or the last artist to make his home there. In the generation before him, Joseph Nollekens, usually reckoned the finest British sculptor of the later eighteenth century, lived for half a century in Mortimer Street. Although he made large sums of money, Nollekens was a notorious miser – when he died, he was found to have only two shoes and they were odd ones. After Constable, a group of painters who referred to themselves as 'The Clique' all had lodgings and studios in Fitzrovia during the late 1830s and early 1840s. The leading lights in the group were WP Frith, Augustus Egg and Richard Dadd. In August 1843, Dadd, whose mental state had been giving his friends and family increasing concern for some time, attacked his father with a knife and razor, killing him. He was incarcerated in the Bethlem mental hospital and his studio in Newman Street was searched. Behind a screen were found portraits of Frith, Egg and other painters of The Clique, all depicted with their throats cut. In the early twentieth century, the Fitzroy Street Group of artists was formed, with Walter Sickert as its leading figure. And, as we have seen, Augustus John was a familiar figure in Fitzrovian streets for much of his life.

In the nineteenth century, writers also flocked to Fitzrovia, largely because it was cheap to rent there. The French poets Paul Verlaine and Arthur Rimbaud lived in Howland Street when they spent time in London in 1872. They advertised themselves as teachers of French, but it seems unlikely they had many, if any, pupils. Most of their days were spent drinking and quarrelling in assorted dives in the neighbourhood. Neither liked the city very much. It was too dark, too muddy and too foggy. The gin, according to Rimbaud, was like 'concentrated sewage water' and Verlaine, like many Frenchmen before and after him, was appalled by English food. Oxtail soup particularly disgusted him. 'Fie on such a horror!' he wrote, 'A man's sock with a rotten clitoris floating in it.'

Some years later, a very different writer took up residence in Fitzrovia. George Bernard Shaw lived in Fitzroy Square. These were the years before his great stage successes and before his marriage to his 'green-eyed millionairess', Charlotte Payne-Townshend. Shaw was living with, and to some extent living off, his mother. 'I did not throw myself into the struggle for life,' he later wrote, 'I threw my mother into it.' It was also during this period that Shaw, a music critic, returned home still thrilled by a ballet performance he had just attended. He began to pirouette around Fitzroy Square in imitation of the dancers he had seen, watched by a policeman who then approached him and asked him what he was doing. When Shaw told him, the officer decided to have a go himself until he fell in the gutter and bloodied his nose. This accident didn't stop a passing milkman from joining in the dancing, but he managed to break his leg while taking his turn around the square and Shaw and the policeman had to carry him off to the nearest hospital.

Like nearby Soho, Fitzrovia was also the haunt of European Communists and anarchists who had found their native lands too hot to hold them and had ended up in London. Lenin, Stalin and Trotsky all spent time there during the first decade of the twentieth century and the Communist Club had its headquarters in Charlotte Street for a time. Charlotte Street was also the setting for the last few days of the Second Congress of the Russian Social Democratic Labour Party and the scene of its fateful division into the Mensheviks and the Bolsheviks, led by Lenin. Twenty years earlier, London had become the new home of Sergey Stepniak, the 'Man of the Steppes', a legendary revolutionary who had assassinated the chief of the Tsar's secret police in St Petersburg in 1878. In Fitzrovia, he established the Society of Friends of Russian Freedom and edited their newsletter. In 1895, Stepniak met an unlikely end for a Russian revolutionary, when he was knocked down and killed by a train on a level crossing at Chiswick. By that time he had already attracted a number of disciples to join him in London, including Wilfrid Voynich, who had escaped from a Siberian prison camp and arrived in the city via a roundabout route involving Beijing, Poland and Hamburg. He became an antiquarian bookseller, with a shop in Shaftesbury Avenue. He is now most famous for the Voynich Manuscript, a medieval codex he claimed to have found in an Italian library, and which is filled with curious illustrations and written in a language that no one has ever been able to decipher.

In the first few decades of the twentieth century, as we have seen, many of the most familiar bohemian haunts, from the Fitzroy Tavern to the Eiffel Tower restaurant, were in what was not yet called Fitzrovia. The list of artists who rented studios in the area is like a roll call of British modernism, from Bloomsbury-associated talents like Roger Fry and Duncan Grant, to old-style bohemians such as Jacob Epstein and Walter Sickert. Throughout the twenties and thirties, Augustus John was a regular in the local pubs, as were Christopher Nevinson and Mark Gertler, one-time members of the Slade's Coster Gang. The maverick Wyndham Lewis, having quarrelled with just about all of his one-time associates, lived in Fitzroy Street and then Percy Street. Surrealists John Banting and Eileen Agar were also Fitzrovian residents. Together with the Hungarian writer Joseph Bard, a friend of Ezra Pound, Agar lived in a ground-floor flat in Fitzroy Square, where, she later wrote, they were very happy, although 'urchins were inclined to piss in our letter box'. Showing a degree of tolerance that others might find difficult to match, she remarked, 'We felt that this was done for the hell of it rather than maliciously, so managed to forgive them so long as no important letters were damaged.'

One of the attractions of the area was that lodgings were cheap, but they could also be insalubrious. 'One Saturday I caught thirty fleas on my leg,' reported the short-story writer and memoirist VS Pritchett, 'and, going to the chemists to buy sulphur candles to kill the plague off, I was told that every chemist in the neighbourhood had sold out.' Other writers who lived and worked in Fitzrovia in the twenties and thirties included WH Auden, Dylan Thomas,

Roy Campbell, who once punched fellow poet Louis MacNeice in the mouth during a heated disagreement in the George pub (MacNeice simply staunched the blood with his handkerchief and remarked, 'There's no need to behave like that, Campbell.') and the literary editor JR Ackerley. When war broke out in 1939 the streets around Fitzroy Square and Charlotte Street were at the centre of cultural life in the capital and they were to remain so throughout the Blitz and beyond.

Bohemia in the Blitz

During the Second World War, Fitzrovia only consolidated its status as London's bohemian heartland. It was not a place where the faint of heart were likely to flourish. 'You had to be quite tough,' the poet John Heath-Stubbs recalled of his youthful days there, 'you had to pay your score – drink quite heavily – you had not to resent it if someone borrowed some money and failed to repay you, and you had to accept a harsh rebuff if one transgressed the unwritten code.' It was also, of course, a place where you could risk your life simply to have a good time. The Blitz meant that death could be the conclusion to a night out. Just across Oxford Street in Soho, the Café de Paris in Coventry Street was destroyed by bombs on the night of 8 March 1941 and dozens of people who had been dining and dancing to the music of Ken 'Snakehips' Johnson and his band were killed. Amongst them was the band leader himself. With cruel irony, the Café, which was underground, had advertised itself as 'the safest place to dance in Town'. (One of the wartime policemen who was among the first on the scene and was shocked both by the decapitated bodies and by the looters who stripped the corpses of their valuables was Ballard Berkeley, later an actor most famous for his role as the Major in *Fawlty Towers*.) Although Fitzrovia was not as hard hit as some areas of the city, it still suffered its share of bombed-out buildings and civilian deaths

THE CAFÉ DE PARIS BOMBING ON THE FRONT PAGE OF THE *DAILY MAIL*,
10 MARCH 1941

during the Blitz. Nonetheless, this 'world of outsiders, down-and-outs, drunks, sensualists, homosexuals and eccentrics', as it was once described, became a home from home for bohemians and pleasure-seekers. Soldiers on leave, especially those with artistic ambitions, flocked to the area's bars and restaurants. In the words of Andrew Sinclair, the Fitzrovians 'bloomed under the blitz and the black-out, conscription and rationing, the fear of sudden death and the snatch at urgent life'.

One of the consequences of the danger was an intense determination to seize any and all opportunities for sex. Why bother with morality and continence when every day could be your last? 'My sexual hunger was avid,' wrote the writer and publisher John Lehmann, 'as it was with so many others at a time when death seemed to tease us with forebodings of liquidations in terrors still undeclared. One curious manifestation of this was in the public urinals. As never before, and with the advantage of the black-out, a number of these, scattered all over London, became notorious for homosexual activities. Heaving bodies filled them, and it was often quite impossible for anyone who genuinely wanted to relieve himself to get in.' According to Quentin Crisp, then an artists' model and café habitué, 'As soon as the bombs started to fall, London became like a paved double-bed. Voices whispered suggestively to you as you walked along; hands reached out if you stood still and in dimly-lit trains people carried on as they had once behaved only in taxis.' On the tube, Crisp was regularly propositioned. 'I was surprised at the frequency with which I found myself sitting opposite some man who between stations decided to try to win fame, like Mr Mercator, for his projection.'

It was not just Lehmann, Crisp and fellow gays who found the Blitz sexually liberating. Joan Wyndham, a young art student and diarist in the early years of the war, had a lucky escape from a bomb. 'If I survive this,' she thought, 'I should go round to Rupert's and get myself de-virginised.' She did exactly that, although she found the experience distinctly underwhelming. 'Goodness, is that all it is?' she confided to her diary. 'I'd rather have a jolly good smoke and go to the pictures any day.' Despite the initial disappointment, Joan spent much of the rest of the war hopping in and out of the beds of her bohemian acquaintances. The writer Peter Quennell later described the intensity of his own sexual feelings during the Blitz. 'Fear and pleasure,' he wrote, 'combined to provoke a mood of wild exhilaration' and 'the impact of a bomb a few hundred yards away only sharpened pleasure's edge.'

Intellectual and artistic life, much of it conducted in the pubs and bars, was similarly intense. 'Never have the London pubs been more stimulating,' Lehmann thought, 'never has one been able to hear more extraordinary revelations, never witness more unlikely encounters.' Few were more stimulating than those in Fitzrovia. The Fitzroy Tavern was still popular, although many people in the know, weary of the tourists who had begun to pitch up there in the hope of brief encounters with *echt* bohemians, had deserted it for other places. Augustus John is supposed to have once remarked that, 'If you haven't visited the Fitzroy, you haven't visited London.' By the forties, too many people agreed with him and the crowds drove many of the true bohemians elsewhere in search of sanctuary. There were plenty of other pubs and clubs they could choose to patronise. The Duke of York in Rathbone Street was run by the so-called 'Mad Major', its landlord Alf Klein, who kept a bugle behind the bar on which he played 'The Last Post' at closing time. Klein demanded of a first-time male customer that he be allowed to snip off the end of his tie and add it to the collection he had accumulated, which grew to number 1,500 in his time as licensee. On one wartime night in the Duke of York, Anthony Burgess's first wife Lynne impressed the hard men of Pirelli's razor gang by her ability to down pints. 'You're a good kid, you are,' she was told. 'If you're ever in trouble with those bastards of O'Flaherty's or the Maltese mob you just call on Pirelli.'

Another pub where violence regularly simmered beneath the surface of social drinking was the Marquis of Granby, also in Rathbone Street. According to Julian Maclaren-Ross, fights broke out there frequently despite the best efforts of the landlord, an ex-policeman, to keep the peace. 'Gigantic guardsmen went there in search of homosexuals to beat up and rob and, finding none, fought instead each other; one summer evening, in broad daylight, a man was savagely killed by several others in a brawl outside while a crowd gathered on the pavement to watch and was dispersed only by the arrival of a squad from Goodge Street Police Station nearby, by which time the killers had made their getaway in someone else's car.' A quieter pub, the Bricklayers Arms in Gresse Street, was better known as the 'Burglar's Rest', because of a (possibly apocryphal) story that a gang of burglars had broken into it one night, downed a prodigious amount of booze, slept off the effects and escaped in the morning before the landlord had realised anything was amiss. The Newman Arms in Rathbone Street was a favourite of George Orwell, who, as a beer drinker, approved of the fact that it only sold that suitably proletarian beverage. It is said to be the model for the 'prole' pub into which Winston Smith ventures in Orwell's *1984*.

The Wheatsheaf was (and still is) in Rathbone Place, just around the corner from the Fitzroy Tavern. Already a haunt of bohemians in the thirties, it was the pub where Augustus John had introduced Caitlin Macnamara, a former chorus girl and model who had briefly been his mistress, to her future husband, Dylan Thomas. As Caitlin later recalled, the Welsh poet 'kind of fell all over me. Put his head on my knee and never stopped talking.' 'Ours was not a love story,' she remarked, 'it was a drink story' and much of the drink was taken on board at the Wheatsheaf. During the war, the pub became ever more popular with writers and their hangers-on. According to Anthony Burgess, future author of *A Clockwork Orange* and then a serving soldier with hopes of becoming a writer, 'To get to the gentlemen's toilets one had to

DYLAN THOMAS AND HIS WIFE CAITLIN THOMAS

fight through a highly literary mob and climb stairs thronged with small poets and their girlfriends.'

The Wheatsheaf became the archetypal pub of Fitzrovian bohemia in the forties, just as the Fitzroy Tavern had been that of the previous decade. Customers included Nina Hamnett, now in her fifties and sinking into jaunty dilapidation. She continued to rattle the tin where she kept her money in front of those who might be prepared to stand her a drink in exchange for her reminiscences about the Parisian art scene of 30 years before. 'Modigliani said I had the best tits in Europe,' she was known to remark before hauling up her clothes to reveal them. 'You feel them. They're as good as new.' By this time, her days as the toast of Parisian and London bohemia long behind her, Hamnett lived in a squalid flat in Howland Street, where the facilities did not run to anything more than a communal toilet shared with other tenants. After the war, in 1947, when the landlady wanted to evict Hamnett and took her to court to do so, she accused the artist of 'misusing' the sink in her room. The magistrate hearing the case was aghast. 'What do you mean,' he is reported to have said, 'a woman urinating in a sink? It's not possible.' Nina's friends, who knew that it was not only possible, but highly likely that she had done exactly what the landlady claimed, were amused by the magistrate's appalled naivety. The case was dismissed, but Hamnett soon moved out and took slightly larger rooms in Westbourne Terrace in Paddington, which she soon rendered equally squalid. She met a memorable, but dreadful, end there in 1956 when, drunk, she either fell or jumped from the window and impaled herself on the area railings below.

A young Quentin Crisp, already dressing to surprise and wearing make-up, found that the Wheatsheaf was one of the few pubs where he was welcome. Even there, he stood out from the crowd. On one occasion the landlord was told by a policeman that he was running 'a funny sort of a place'. When the landlord asked, 'How funny?', the policeman merely gestured in the direction of Crisp. Philip O'Connor, Jim Phelan and John Gawsworth were other Wheatsheaf regulars. O'Connor, the product of a wildly unconventional upbringing which he later recorded in the 1958 bestseller *Memoirs of a Public Baby*, had been a peripheral figure in London bohemia since his teenage years in the early thirties. Unstable and often close to mental illness, he declaimed his verse in public bars until he was ejected from them. He would also stand for hours at Hyde Park Corner, roaring out intense if not always coherent statements of his ideas about art and politics. Even his ordinary speech was eccentric, filled with spoonerisms, jingles and sentences spoken backwards, and he was frequently drunk. His surrealist-influenced poetry was published in magazines such as Geoffrey Grigson's *New Verse*, but O'Connor had little time for most other poets and had a penchant for playing semi-demented pranks on famous authors. He sent a note to Aldous Huxley in a hotel room, demanding a £5 note with menaces, and once startled TS Eliot by jumping out from behind a door and yelling 'Boo!' very loudly in the great man's face.

JOHN GAWSWORTH, POET, EDITOR, BIBLIOGRAPHER AND THIRD KING OF
REDONDA, SEEN HERE KNIGHTING VISCOUNT ST DAVIDS ON BARGE, 1950s

The Irish republican Jim Phelan was sentenced to death for
his part in a robbery in 1924 that ended in murder, but he had
his sentence commuted to life imprisonment, of which he served
13 years. By the war years he was earning a living as a writer of
books about his experiences as a prisoner and, later, as a tramp.
John Gawsworth, born in 1912, was a poet, anthologist and, later,
King of Redonda. He had been working in determined opposition
to modernism since the 1930s. He favoured 'traditional' verse and
championed obscure and forgotten authors such as MP Shiel, writer
of *The Purple Cloud*, a sub-Wellsian 'scientific romance' about the
last man on earth, which had first been published in 1901. Shiel
died in 1947, having made Gawsworth his literary executor. Shiel
bequeathed Gawsworth the title of King of Redonda, a guano-
strewn islet in the Caribbean, which Shiel's father had supposedly
owned and bestowed upon his son in the 1880s. Gawsworth kept

some of Shiel's ashes in a canister in his flat and was reputed sometimes to sprinkle a few as seasoning into the stews he cooked.

Another outpost of artistic life during the war centred on a number of pubs near Broadcasting House in Portland Place, which became, in the words of Robert Hewison, 'a miniature BBC bohemia', where employees of the broadcaster and freelancers in search of work from them congregated. The busiest of these was the George, which had been earlier dubbed 'the Gluepot' by the conductor Sir Henry Wood, because he had such difficulty getting his orchestra members out of it when they were needed to play at the nearby Queen's Hall. The name had, appropriately enough, stuck. Here composers like Constant Lambert and Elisabeth Lutyens rubbed shoulders and downed drinks in the company of writers, artists and producers from the BBC's Third Programme, such as RD Smith, husband of the novelist Olivia Manning, and the poet Louis MacNeice. Other neighbouring pubs such as the Stag's Head and the Horse and Groom in Great Portland Street, sometimes known as 'the Whore's Lament' (supposedly because of the despair expressed by the local tarts when free-spending American servicemen returned home at the end of the war), were also popular. Further out of town, the Old Swan in Notting Hill Gate was a regular Sunday meeting place for painters because it was close to the studio used by the so-called 'Two Roberts', Robert Colquhoun and Robert MacBryde, and (for a time) by John Minton.

The Scottish painters, Robert Colquhoun and Robert MacBryde, lovers and artistic collaborators, were archetypal examples of the artists of varying degrees of dissoluteness, eccentricity and talent who filled these Fitzrovian pubs throughout the war years. They had met one another as teenagers at the Glasgow School of Art in 1932 and they stayed together until Colquhoun's death 30 years later. After a period of travelling in France and Italy before the war and several unhappy months in which Colquhoun served in the Royal Army Medical Corps after the conflict began, they arrived

THE PAINTERS COLQUHOUN & MCBRYDE (THE TWO ROBERTS),
IAN FLEMING, 1937-38

in London in the spring of 1941 and very quickly established themselves as belligerent boozers on the Fitzrovian circuit. Once drink had been taken they were quarrelsome, quick to take offence and often outrageously offensive. 'What d'you think about when you're sober?,' the writer Julian Maclaren-Ross once asked MacBryde. 'Do you prepare apologies for the people you've been rude to the night before?' 'Maybe I'm thinking up a new lot of rude things to say next time I'm drunk,' MacBryde replied.

Colquhoun was equally formidable when drunk. According to the poet Dom Moraes, who met him in the 1950s, he was 'terrifying in his cups; his thin body seemed to buckle forwards at the hips, while his legs weaved a wild way across the floor. In a thunderous, bullying voice, his eyes unfocused, he would demand to be bought a drink.' The two men were also famous for the raging arguments they had together. Many of these were the consequence of the bisexual Colquhoun's persistent interest in the opposite sex. MacBryde was said to ration his lover to one woman a month and was even rumoured to lie occasionally under the bed while such encounters took place, sarcastically commenting on what was going on between the sheets. When they were invited by Anthony Cronin to stay overnight at his house in Wembley, they proved lively guests, with a naked Colquhoun chasing an equally naked MacBryde through the front gardens of the street, brandishing a carving knife, while a thunderstorm raged overhead. During the war and immediately afterwards, both painters, but particularly Colquhoun, were much admired and their work was sought after, but the fifties proved a difficult decade for them. They were devastated both personally and professionally when thieves broke into their studio and destroyed all the paintings there. On the night of 20 September 1962, Colquhoun was working in the studio when he suffered a massive heart attack and died in his friend's arms. MacBryde never truly recovered from his loss. Four years later, he was drunkenly dancing outside a Dublin pub when he was knocked down by a passing car and killed.

Poets and writers by the dozens drank and socialised in wartime Fitzovia. There was Paul Potts, poet and sometime friend of George Orwell, who touted his self-printed verse around the pubs of the area and once stole the young Iris Murdoch's typewriter, arguing that his need for it was greater than hers. Gerald Kersh led a varied career as bodyguard, debt collector, French teacher, wrestler and cinema manager – and wrote *Night and the City*, one of the most insightful novels about Soho life in the 1930s. George Barker, now half-forgotten, but once acclaimed as a genius by the likes of TS Eliot and WB Yeats, lived the romantic ideal of the flamboyant, irresponsible poet even more thoroughly than his contemporary Dylan Thomas, drinking prodigiously and flitting back and forth between a series of female lovers. He went on to father fifteen children by four different women.

Ruthven Todd was a Scottish-born poet and novelist who was an expert on William Blake, a surrealist at the time of the 1936 International Surrealist Exhibition and a conscientious objector during the war. According to the anarchist thinker and literary critic George Woodcock, 'he was the great go-between of literary London in those days' and seemed to know everybody who was anybody in that world. Todd also provides us with one memorable anecdote, which is almost a summation of bohemia in the Blitz. He was walking in Dean Street late one night in 1942. 'In the light of a parachute-flare dropped by a German plane,' he reports in his introduction to the catalogue of an exhibition entitled *Fitzrovia and the Road to York Minster*, 'I saw a most peculiarly flaccid tripod approaching me from the north. The legs wobbled and wove and crumpled and it was clear that it was only possible for the three persons to move as a tripod linked by arms over one another's shoulders. The tripod seemed unaware of the air-raid and of the nasty sharp splinters of ack-ack shrapnel that were pitter-pattering down in the streets. I remained in the shadow of the Highlander waiting for a lull in the gunfire and stayed there as the tripod wobbled past. The three legs were Augustus John, Nina Hamnett and Norman Douglas, all three, to use an expressive Mallorcan phrase, as drunk as sponges, on their way to the Gargoyle for an unneeded drink.'

Two Exemplary Fitzrovians

The inseparable Roberts, as well as individuals like Ruthven Todd and Paul Potts, John Gawsworth and Philip O'Connor, were characteristic inhabitants of 1940s Fitzrovia, but two men more than any others exemplified the place and the period. One was Dylan Thomas, who had first made his mark in the previous decade. The other was Julian Maclaren-Ross. Although he was two years older than Thomas, and had occasionally drunk in its pubs in the 1930s, Maclaren-Ross did not properly arrive in Fitzrovia until the war years. Once he did so, he rapidly became one of its most distinctive denizens. Attired in his usual outfit of a smart suit and camel-hair coat, a carnation in his buttonhole, a cigarette holder between his teeth and mirror sunglasses hiding his eyes, he clutched his trademark silver-topped malacca cane in his hand as he propped up the bar in the Wheatsheaf.

Unsurprisingly, in the limited confines of wartime Fitzrovia, the two men knew one another. Indeed, they worked together for a while at Strand Films in Soho. Their first assignment, improbably, was to construct a script based on the activities of the Home Guard. Julian Maclaren-Ross described the young poet as dressed in 'a very respectable dark blue suit and a white shirt with a bow tie and celluloid collar, too tight around the neck and giving the effect of someone strapped in the stocks. In these clothes he might have been a young provincial tradesman or perhaps a farmer up in London for the day on business.' When they both retired for a drink at the end of their first day at Strand, Thomas proved even more scathing about Maclaren-Ross's own appearance and particularly the silver-topped malacca cane. 'Fucking dandy,' he remarked. 'Flourishing that stick. Why don't you try to look more sordid? Sordidness, boy, that's the thing.'

Thomas, of course, knew a thing or two about sordidness. The 'Rimbaud of Cwmdonkin Drive', as he called himself, was born in Swansea in 1914 and began to write poetry as a schoolboy. His first volume, *18 Poems*, was published in 1934. This was also the year in which he decided (in the words of Hugh David) that 'it was not easy to live the *vie de bohème* in suburban Swansea'. Encouraged by the interest of the eccentric Victor Neuburg, a former associate of occultist Aleister Crowley, who published some of Thomas's poems in 'Poets' Corner', the column he edited in a Sunday newspaper, Thomas moved to London and embarked on a precarious career as a freelance writer and broadcaster. Publication of further

POET DYLAN THOMAS PICTURED AT HIS FLAT IN CHELSEA, LONDON, 1945

collections of his verse made his reputation as the most gifted and innovative poet of the younger generation. Rapidly establishing a parallel reputation for flamboyant behaviour and heavy drinking, he soon set a pattern for the rest of his career. Weeks of booze and relentless socialising in the pubs and drinking clubs of the capital ('too much talk, too much drink, too many girls', as Dylan himself described it) would alternate with country retreats to recover his shattered health and to write his poetry. Returning to London, he would always mean to continue his literary work, but, as he wrote in a letter of 1936, 'When I do come to town, bang go my plans in a horrid alcoholic explosion that scatters all my good intentions like bits of limbs and clothes over the doorsteps and into the saloon bars of the tawdriest pubs in London.' The pattern continued throughout the war years and beyond.

Innumerable accounts of Dylan's boozy odysseys through the London night have been published. One of the oddest is by

Gerald Kersh, who describes Dylan on a bender with the novelist Philip Lindsay. 'Dylan,' Kersh records, 'got his penis stuck in a two ounce honey pot. Why he put it there I don't know. On the same occasion he pushed a shirt button up his nose and couldn't get it out either.' When not in search of his next pint, or indeed his next two-ounce honey pot, Dylan was equally relentless in pursuit of sex. Few women were safe from his drunken advances. The diarist and former art student Joan Wyndham, by then in uniform as a member of the WAAF (Women's Auxiliary Air Force), gives a vivid account of his unsubtle attempts to seduce her in 1943. The poet had introduced himself in the Wheatsheaf with the words, 'I'm Dylan Thomas and I'm fucking skint. Be nice to me, Waafie, and buy me another Special Ale.' On a later pub crawl, she found herself in a taxi with Thomas on the way to Ruthven Todd's flat near the British Museum. 'As soon as I'd sunk into my seat Dylan smothered me in wet beery kisses,' she wrote, 'his blubbery tongue forcing my lips apart. It was rather like being embraced by an intoxicated octopus. I tried to tell myself that I was being kissed by a great poet but it was a relief when the taxi finally stopped.' They both decided to stay at Todd's and Wyndham retired to sleep in the spare room, wisely bolting the door. She was just dozing off when she was awakened by a fumbling at the door and Dylan chanting outside, 'I want to fuck you! I want to fuck you!' The door remained bolted.

Until recently it seemed as if Maclaren-Ross was fated to be forgotten, or remembered only as the model for the doomed novelist X Trapnel in Anthony Powell's *Dance to the Music of Time*. In the last 20 years, however, his genuine talents as a short-story writer and as a self-mythologising memoirist have begun to be recognised. He was born in South Norwood in 1912, but spent much of his childhood and adolescence in France. Returning to England in the thirties, he lived in a series of cheap hotels and boarding houses in south-coast seaside resorts, embarked on a brief and unsuccessful marriage with a would-be actress, earned a precarious living as a door-to-door vacuum salesman and tried to kickstart a literary career by adapting novels he admired into radio plays for the BBC. After a disastrous spell as a soldier, which ended in a stay in a military psychiatric hospital near Birmingham, he was discharged from the army and began to publish his short fiction in wartime magazines like *Horizon* and *New Writing*. Gravitating inevitably to Fitzrovia, he took up residence in its pubs and drinking clubs.

His favourite watering-hole by far was the Wheatsheaf pub, where he surrounded himself with an ever-changing entourage of cronies and acolytes, which included, at various times, the poet and publisher Charles Wrey Gardiner, the New Zealand writer Dan Davin, the young and learned poet John Heath-Stubbs and the novelist Peter Vansittart. The Eurasian writer Noel Sircar, another Wheatsheaf disciple, would one day publish an anthropomorphic children's book in which Maclaren-Ross and his famous malacca cane provided the inspiration for a character called Bertram the Badger. Standing in his preferred position at the bar, Maclaren-Ross would hold forth at great length on his pet subjects, demonstrating the astonishingly detailed recall he had for the novels and films which he admired.

By the last years of the war, Maclaren-Ross had become a legend in his own lunchtime. His daily routine has been described by plenty of chroniclers of the period, but by none so succinctly as Dan Davin: 'Midday in the pub till closing time, a late lunch in the Scala restaurant in Charlotte Street, roast beef with as much fat as possible and lashings of horseradish sauce, a stroll to look at the bookshops in Charing Cross Road and to buy Royalty, his special jumbo-sized cigarettes. Opening time again at the Wheatsheaf till closing time. A hurried dash to the Highlander, which closed half an hour later. Back to the Scala for supper and coffee. At midnight the tube home from Goodge Street.'

How Maclaren-Ross managed to do any writing amidst all this may seem a mystery. The mystery becomes slightly less baffling when one realises that he was using drugs to stimulate all-night writing sessions after he had returned from Soho and Fitzrovia to whatever temporary digs he was inhabiting. Benzedrine was obtained from inhalers intended for asthma sufferers; methedrine capsules – what he called his 'green bombs' – were prescribed by a shady doctor who drank in the Wheatsheaf.

Maclaren-Ross's own account of wartime bohemia can be found in *Memoirs of the Forties*, vividly quirky reminiscences of his heyday which remained unfinished at the time of his death. What he had managed to put on paper was published in book form the following year. One of the most memorable portraits in Maclaren-Ross's memoirs is that of the Tamil poet and editor Tambi, a defining figure of the Fitzrovian forties, whom Maclaren-Ross met for the first time in the Helvetia, always known as the Swiss Tavern, in Old Compton Street. Meary James Tambimuttu, known to everyone as 'Tambi', was born in what was then Ceylon in 1915 and came to London when he was in his early twenties. Gravitating to the pubs of Soho and Fitzrovia, he rapidly established himself in the capital's literary life. He founded *Poetry London* in 1939 and, throughout the war years, this was one of the most interesting and exciting magazines available, publishing a wide range of writers from Dylan Thomas and Lawrence Durrell to Louis MacNeice and Kathleen Raine. TS Eliot said of it that, 'It is only in *Poetry London* that I can consistently expect to find new poets who matter.' However, the magazine, plagued by financial crises, appeared only intermittently and Tambi himself was notoriously disorganised. Manuscripts, some of them nibbled by passing rats, piled up in the corners of *Poetry London*'s squalid office and, on one occasion, a handwritten poem by Dylan Thomas was fished out of the huge Victorian chamber pot which Tambi used as an improvised filing cabinet. As an editor, Tambi was just as likely to borrow money from his contributors as he was to pay them. Maclaren-Ross records a conversation with him soon after they had been introduced:

> 'Do you have any money?'
> 'Yes, thank you. I've got £5.'
> 'That is good,' Tambimuttu said. 'I am a Prince in my country and princes don't carry money, you know. Give me the fiver and later the firm will refund you. I am going to lunch with TS Eliot. You know who is TS Eliot?'

Tambi pocketed the fiver and went for lunch with Eliot. Maclaren-Ross, needless to say, was never repaid.

Tambi was, in his idiosyncratic way, a patron of both poets and painters. The artist Gerald Wilde was one of the recipients of his dubious largesse. Maclaren-Ross records one occasion when Tambi passes a hat around the Wheatsheaf. 'I am setting up a fund for Gerald Wilde the Mad Artist,' he tells the drinkers. 'He's starving and with no money, you know.' People contribute to the fund with varying degrees of generosity. The money, of course, never reaches Wilde, who has been despatched to Tambi's flat, with strict instructions to get painting, but instead is spent on drinks and food for the editor and his entourage. Maclaren-Ross tells of another time when Tambi locked 'the Mad Artist' in his flat to work and then left for a weekend in the country, forgetting all about him. When he returned it was to discover that Wilde, maddened by hunger and the need for a drink, had smashed through the door to the outside world and disappeared into the night with a pile of Tambi's most valuable books. These he had sold to a bookshop and spent the proceeds in the pub. Wilde has often been described as the real-life model for Gully Jimson, the artist anti-hero of Joyce Cary's novel *The Horse's Mouth*, although, since painter and novelist didn't meet until five years after the book's publication, this seems unlikely. Wilde was, in the words of one writer, 'an old-style Soho drunk', who could regularly be found 'yelling and screeching' in pubs and 'giving away pictures for drinking money'. He was also an original and gifted artist whose work is long overdue for rediscovery.

In the fifties, which he described as 'a decade... I could have well done without', Maclaren-Ross's fortunes went rapidly downhill. His capacity to continue working in the most difficult of circumstances was severely tested, as he struggled with debt, eviction, occasional homelessness and the vexing unwillingness of publishers to stump up advances for books which were much promised, but only rarely delivered. He churned out book reviews for newspapers and magazines, parodies of favourite writers for *Punch* and radio scripts, but he found it impossible to produce the great novel he was always telling himself and others he would write. He entered the new decade of the sixties in poor health and poor morale. In 1964, he began to write instalments of *Memoirs of the Forties*, but he suffered a heart attack before he was able to finish the book as he planned it and died in November of that year. The book was published the following year by Alan Ross, who described it accurately as 'the front-line account of bohemian wartime Soho by its longest serving combatant'. Others, unsurprisingly, were less complimentary. Tambimuttu, by then living in the USA, called it 'a highly coloured book of misrepresentations and fairy tales'.

Maclaren-Ross and Dylan Thomas were very different figures to the Bloomsburyites and the Bright Young Things. In some ways, they seemed like throwbacks to the original London bohemians of the 1850s and 1860s, men like George Augustus Sala and the Brough brothers. They were professional writers, struggling daily to make a living in a difficult market, and spending much of what they earned in pubs and alehouses. Yet they were also pointers towards the future. In retrospect, Thomas in particular seems, as Hugh David wrote, 'the precursor of a new breed of bohemian'.

He was not, as so many in previous generations were, someone turning his back on privilege and a private income. He was lower middle-class and provincial in his origins. As the war ended and the fifties beckoned, he was the avatar of many bohemians yet to come. And their stamping ground was to be Soho.

Chapter Seven

SOHO AND
THE FIFTIES

'Only Soho is bohemia.'
ARTHUR SYMONS, *The Café Royal and Other Essays*

A Short History of Bohemian Soho

B Y THE 1950s, Soho had already been a bohemian stronghold for a long time. First developed in the late seventeenth century, it was originally the resort of the rich and aristocratic. For most of its history it has also been one of the capital's more cosmopolitan areas. As early as 1711, about two-fifths of the population of the parish of St Anne's, Soho was French and, 30 years later, one writer was of the opinion that, 'Many parts of this parish so greatly abound with French that is an easy matter for a stranger to imagine himself in France.' In the centuries that followed, the neighbourhood became home to generations of immigrants from other parts of Europe. A survey in the 1890s found Germans, French, Italians, Poles, Russians, Swiss, Swedes and even a handful of Persians, all living in Soho.

Throughout its history it has also garnered a reputation for rackety behaviour and the pursuit of pleasure. This was as true in the middle of the eighteenth century as it was in the middle of the twentieth. Madame Cornelys, an Austrian who had once been Casanova's lover, pitched up in London in 1759 and rented Carlisle House in Soho Square. There she held a series of balls, masquerades and musical recitals which, over the next decade and more, became the most fashionable events in town, not least because they were famous as meeting places for sex. 'The whole design of the libidinous assembly,' sniffed one disapproving witness of a Cornelys party, 'seems to terminate in assignations and intrigues.' Given their opportunities for disguise and covert liaisons, the masquerade parties were particularly popular. In February 1770, nearly 800 people crammed into Carlisle House and several thousand more lined the neighbouring streets to watch them arrive. Guests competed to create the most memorable costumes. One MP turned up dressed in a shroud and carrying a coffin. Another, like some eccentric competitor in the modern London Marathon, appeared as a thatched cottage, his head just visible through a window. Most sensational of all was that of a certain Captain Watson of the Guards, who arrived as the biblical Adam. 'The unavoidable indelicacy of the dress, flesh-coloured silk with an apron of fig leaves worked in it, fitting the body to the utmost nicety, rendered it the contempt of the whole company,' reported one contemporary. One suspects that, if Captain Watson had any sort of figure, there may have been as much admiration as contempt directed towards him.

It was also at one of Madame Cornelys's masquerades that roller skates were first demonstrated to the London public. The clock-maker John Joseph Merlin made his appearance at the party gliding across the floor on boots which he had adapted by fitting them with wheels. Playing the violin as he flew across the floor on his wheel-driven boots, Merlin made a big impression on the fashionable crowd there, but disaster struck. Unfortunately, he had omitted to include either brakes or a means of steering in his design for his skates and, in the words of a contemporary report, Merlin 'impelled himself against a mirror of more than £500 value, dashed it to atoms, broke his instrument to pieces and wounded himself severely'. Madame Cornelys herself was in and out of debtors' prison throughout the 1770s, eventually lost control of Carlisle House and, after a chequered later career which involved at different times running a hotel in Southampton, selling asses' milk in Knightsbridge and escaping from the King's Bench Prison in Southwark when it was set on fire by the Gordon Rioters, she died in the Fleet Prison in 1797, aged 74. A friend who witnessed her death later wrote that she found her, 'sitting up in bed with a large crucifix exclaiming in a voice that denoted the most dreadful horror, "The devil is dragging me down" which she kept constantly repeating' until she 'expired in the most shocking agonies'.

By the first decade of the nineteenth century, Soho was already a destination for artistically minded young men in flight from their upbringings. It was there that the 17-year-old Thomas De Quincey spent much of his time on the streets in 1802 after he had deserted his home and family in Manchester. He slept in shop doorways, took temporary shelter in a house in Greek Street and befriended a young prostitute named Anne. As the older De Quincey told the story in his book *Confessions of an English Opium Eater*, Anne saved his life after he collapsed, faint with hunger, on the steps of a house in Soho Square. She cared for him and nursed him back to health. Some weeks later, De Quincey left the city for a while and arranged to meet Anne on his return. She didn't put in an appearance on the appointed night, or on any of the other nights on which he waited at the meeting place. He never saw her again.

In the spring of 1811, 19-year-old Percy Bysshe Shelley and his friend Thomas Hogg, newly sent down from Oxford for writing a pamphlet entitled *The Necessity of Atheism*, arrived in Soho and took lodgings in Poland Street. 'We must stay here, stay for ever', the poet told his companion and was unaccountably delighted by the wallpaper in his room, which was covered by images of vines and grapes. The excitable Shelley took to striding through Soho streets in search of adventure, surviving largely on a diet of hunks of bread and raisins, which he bought loose from a grocery shop and kept in his pockets. In the event, he and Hogg stayed not for ever but for a few weeks, although a blue plaque now marks the site of their sojourn in the street. Instead, the poet eloped to Scotland with his 16-year-old girlfriend Harriet Westbrook, where they married, much to the consternation of both their families.

As the nineteenth century continued, Soho became increasingly impoverished. Large areas of it were overcrowded and breeding grounds for disease. It was in Broad Street, now Broadwick Street, in 1854 that the physician John Snow was able to prove that a particular water pump was the source of a severe cholera outbreak, thus adding to the mounting evidence he was accumulating that the disease was waterborne, rather than the result of 'miasmas' or 'bad air', as conventional wisdom had it. It was about this time that Karl Marx was living with his wife and children in a two-roomed attic flat in Dean Street, rented from an Italian cook named Giovanni Marengo. Although Marx was receiving financial assistance from his friend Friedrich Engels and earning a little as a journalist, the family were as poor as most of their neighbours. 'There is not one piece of good, solid furniture in the entire flat,' one visitor reported. 'Everything is broken, tattered and torn, finger-thick dust everywhere, and everything in the greatest disorder; a large, old-fashioned table, covered with waxcloth, stands in the middle of the drawing-room, on it lie manuscripts, books, newspapers, then the children's toys, bits and pieces of the woman's sewing things, next to it a few teacups with broken rims, dirty spoons, knives, forks, candlesticks, inkpot, glasses, dutch clay pipes, tobacco-ash, in a word all kinds of trash...

Everything is dirty, everything covered in dust; it is dangerous to sit down.' It is little wonder that Marx escaped whenever he could to the British Museum Reading Room to work. His wife Jenny was not so lucky, although it was an inheritance from her Prussian aristocratic family that eventually allowed them to move to better accommodation in Kentish Town. By the time they did so, the Marxes had endured the deaths of three of their children.

Marx's archetypally bohemian habits were noted by the same observer who had been taken aback by the filth in his flat. 'Though he is often idle for days on end, he will work day and night with tireless endurance when he has a great deal of work to do. He has no fixed times for going to sleep and waking up. He often stays up all night and then lies down fully clothed on the sofa at midday and sleeps till evening.' One of the reasons Marx may have had for sleeping on the sofa all afternoon was that he'd had far too much to drink the night before. He was, on occasion, a prodigious boozer and his fellow German, the founder of the Social Democratic Party, Wilhelm Liebknecht, records an epic pub crawl up Tottenham Court Road in the 1850s. After refreshing themselves in a wide variety of alehouses, Marx, Liebknecht and another German exile named Edgar Bauer ended up in the backroom of one particular dive with a group of English clubmen known as Oddfellows. Friendly banter about the respective virtues of the English and the German nations descended into a near brawl when Bauer accused the Oddfellows of 'English cant' and the three Germans exited into the street in the early hours of the morning. There they stumbled over a pile of paving stones and decided that the best thing they could do was to throw them at the street lights. They smashed four or five and the noise attracted the attention of a policeman on the beat. He blew on his whistle, which brought several of his colleagues to the scene. Marx, Liebknecht and Bauer legged it through the streets and alleyways of Fitzrovia with the police in hot pursuit.

The future author of *Das Kapital* knew the area better than the police officers and led his friends to safety.

Soho continued to be noted for its cosmopolitanism throughout the rest of the nineteenth century. In a travel guide of 1902 entitled *Living London*, it was described as 'the cherished home of foreign artists, dancers, musicians, and singers… and the sanctuary of political refugees, conspirators, deserters, and defaulters of all nations'. Soho also had a reputation as a hotbed of criminality. Greek Street was denounced as the 'worst street in the West End of London' by a police officer giving evidence to a Royal Commission in 1906, who alleged that 'some of the vilest reptiles in London live there or frequent it'. It was seen as a place where vice thrived and virtue was shunned.

Foreign anarchists were supposedly everywhere in Soho and they met regularly, according to an article in one scaremongering magazine, *Cassell's Saturday Journal*, in 1900 'to discuss the most diabolical plots of revenge on society'. In the words of another article, written for a newspaper four years earlier, these dangerous agitators spoke 'a sort of mongrel, bestial dialect, more fit for the lips of gorillas and chimpanzees… a sort of reeking hotch-potch of obscene, and often quite meaningless expression'. The paranoia and xenophobia communicated in the press did have some kind of roots in reality. Like its northern neighbour Fitzrovia, Soho had more than its fair share of political radicals and activists, many of them exiles from the Continent and some of them committed to violence to attain their ends. In 1894, Martial Bourdin, a French ladies' tailor working in Soho and living in Fitzroy Street, was killed when he tripped in Greenwich Park and the bomb he was carrying to plant in the Royal Observatory blew up prematurely. The incident was one of the influences on Joseph Conrad's 1907 novel *The Secret Agent*, in which Verloc, half-hearted anarchist and owner of a seedy pornography shop in Soho, is forced into a bomb plot very similar to Bourdin's.

Pubs and Clubs

Throughout the first decades of the twentieth century, Soho remained, in imagination and (to a great extent) in reality, a place of both danger and delight. It was an area that held the promise of sexual freedom and pleasure on the one hand, and violence and criminality on the other. As the writer Thomas Burke remarked, 'When the respectable Londoner wants to feel devilish he goes to Soho.'

However, it was during the 1950s that Soho had its heyday and developed the reputation for sleazy glamour which clings to it still. In the words of London historian Ed Glinert, 'In a grey era of austerity, conformity, rationing and increasing state involvement, Soho meant louche, loose, licentious living.' It was a place where sex and music, drink and drugs, oddballs and artists, could all be found. It was home to the famous Windmill Theatre, where nudity was allowed as long as the women who posed naked in *tableaux vivants* remained motionless. 'If it moves, it's rude' was the motto as the Windmill Girls displayed their all. Many of the best-known comedians of later decades, from Tony Hancock and Peter Sellers to Tommy Cooper and Bruce Forsyth, had their first real successes telling jokes in the brief intervals when female flesh was not on display, although it's fair to assume that few of the punters at the Windmill came to see the comics. Soho was where the British film industry had its heartland on Wardour Street. And, in an age when British cuisine was at its lowest ebb, Soho was one of the few places where good food could be found and restaurants like Wheelers, Kettner's and Quo Vadis thrived. 'The fifties were a time of austerity,' George Melly wrote, 'of punitive conventions, of a grey uniformity... Soho was perhaps the only area in London where the rules didn't apply. It was a bohemian no-go area, tolerance its password, where bad behaviour was cherished – at any rate, in retrospect. Only bores were made unwelcome.'

THE WINDMILL THEATRE, 1958

Fifties Soho was home to a whole tribe of eccentrics and misfits, the most notable of whom was probably Iron Foot Jack, the self-styled 'King of the Bohemians'. Australian-born Jack Neave (sometimes Nieve) had, at some time in his past, had an accident which shortened his right leg by some six inches. To compensate, he wore a metal device on his boot which gave him his nickname. Over the years he provided a number of explanations of his accident. He had been caught in an avalanche in Tibet. He had been shot during a smuggling expedition. He told George Melly that he had lost part of his leg to a shark, although, as Melly points out, this seemed 'an unlikely explanation as he had retained the foot itself'. Even without his iron boot, Jack was a distinctive figure. Bald on the top of his head, with long white locks flowing down the sides on to his shoulders, he was usually dressed in a velvet jacket and a cravat with a jewelled pin. He spent his days roaming the cafés and bars of Soho, offering trinkets for sale and handing out handwritten copies of his own poems.

By the fifties, Iron Foot Jack was little more than a vagrant with a habit of hinting at the strange occult powers he possessed, but, 20 years earlier, he had run the Caravan, a gay-friendly club in Endell Street, which had attracted police attention as 'a sink of iniquity', only frequented, according to an anonymous informant, by 'sexual perverts, lesbians and sodomites'. Arrests had been made after an undercover constable reported mostly male couples dancing and that he had been engaged in conversation by a man who insisted his name was Josephine. In the ensuing trial, Neave denied that the dancing in the club was 'indecent' in any way and a professional dancer called Carmen Fernandez was called as an expert witness to testify that the Rumba, which had apparently appalled the police when they raided the club, was nothing more than a recent craze introduced from the USA. Carmen was all prepared to demonstrate the Rumba for the court, but the judge intervened. 'There will be nothing of the sort in this court,' he firmly stated. In the end, Neave was sentenced to 20 months' hard labour, but most of the rest of those arrested were either given very short sentences or released.

Back in Fitzrovia, just across Oxford Street, life continued to revolve around its pubs. The Fitzroy Tavern, in addition to those bohemian survivors of the 1930s and 1940s who remained faithful to it, now had some unlikely customers. Bob Fabian, a police detective so famous in his time that he had a BBC crime series, *Fabian of the Yard*, named after him, drank there. So too did the public executioner Albert Pierrepoint, who was a frequent visitor to the pub when down in London on official business. (When the landlord and landlady Charles and Annie Allchild organised a party for local children, Pierrepoint proved one of the most popular of the regulars who lent a hand. 'Hangman Brings Life to

Party' one newspaper headline read the following day.) Neither of these two upholders of the law proved particularly helpful in 1955 when the Allchilds were brought before the Magistrates' Court in Marlborough Street, accused of allowing disorderly conduct in the Fitzroy. Undercover police in the pub had allegedly witnessed attempts by 'perverted' customers, some with dyed hair, rouged cheeks and high, effeminate voices, to seduce innocent members of the armed forces who were also drinking there. Arms had been linked, buttocks had been touched and thighs had been fondled. A hand had even been thrust up the kilt of a Seaforth Highlander. Assignations had been made in the gentlemen's toilets. On another occasion ladies of the street were said to be soliciting on the premises. One had approached a policeman in plain clothes and asked him: 'Are you looking for a naughty girl or a naughty boy?' 'Neither', the flustered PC had replied. Seen from the perspective of 2017, the case seems largely ridiculous, but it was no joke at the time. Charles Allchild was found guilty on nine of the counts brought against him and fined. Although he was later acquitted on appeal, the strain of the trial was undoubtedly one of the major reasons he and his wife retired from running the Fitzroy the following year.

Life in 1950s Soho also revolved around the pubs. Perhaps the most famous of them all, celebrated in so many of the memoirs of the period, was the York Minster, always known as the French House, in Dean Street. It had opened originally in 1891 and was run by a German named Schmidt, but, after his death, the licence passed first to his widow and then to Victor Berlemont. Like Agatha Christie's Hercule Poirot, Victor had an impressive moustache and was usually assumed to be French when, in fact, he was Belgian. After Victor's death, the French House was taken over by his equally moustachioed son Gaston, who had been born in an upstairs room in the pub in 1914, the year his father took it over. It was patronised by the so-called 'Fifis', well-dressed prostitutes who either were, or claimed to be, French. Gaston Berlemont remembered them as 'lovely girls – the best in the world. They used to come in here and have a half-bottle of champagne, a Pernod or a Ricard. And if anyone approached them, they'd yell for help. They might promptly leave here and go and stand on their corner, or wherever it was they worked. But in here was sacred. I'd tell the men to hop it.' During the Second World War the French House was popular with the Free French forces in London and even General de Gaulle was known to patronise it. Unlike most, if not all, other British pubs at the time, the French House treated beer as a less important drink than wine. Beer could only be bought in half-pints, whereas the Berlemonts offered a wide range of good wines by the glass as well as by the bottle. Throughout the forties and fifties and beyond, it was also the haunt of poets and painters. Everyone who was anyone in Soho bohemia, from Tambimuttu and Dylan Thomas to Francis Bacon and Henrietta Moraes, drank there. It was at the French House that a drunken Dylan Thomas accidentally left the original manuscript of *Under Milk Wood* beneath his chair and then departed shortly afterwards for America. Gaston Berlemont rescued it and kept it until BBC radio producer Douglas Cleverdon managed to track it down and take possession of it.

The Pillars of Hercules in Greek Street was where the 1890s poet Francis Thompson, overcome by drink and opium, was found by his benefactor Wilfred Meynell slumped in a doorway. Meynell rescued Thompson from his life on the street and undertook to publish his poetry. (In the 1970s the Pillars was to become the haunt of writers such as Martin Amis, Ian McEwan and Clive James, who were associated with Ian Hamilton's magazine *The New Review*.) Other well-known Soho pubs included the Highlander in Dean Street; the Intrepid Fox in Wardour Street; the Macclesfield, which changed its name in 1959 to De Hems, after a nineteenth-century Dutch sea captain who had once been its landlord and became a haunt of people in the music business in the 1960s, hustling their records into the Top Twenty over whisky and cokes in the pub's Oyster Bar; and the Coach and Horses, also in Greek Street, famous for its later associations with *Private Eye* magazine and with the legendarily dissipated Jeffrey Bernard, and for its tenant, Norman Balon, reputedly the 'rudest landlord in London'.

Some cafés and restaurants gained their own notoriety. The Coffee An' (sometimes corrupted into the Café Ann) seems to have derived its name from the fact that you could get coffee an' something else there – usually nothing more than a cheap steak and a salami sandwich. It was reputed to be the cheapest place to eat in Soho and attracted a richly varied array of customers. One of its regulars was the semi-deranged Count Potocki of Montalk, who had once been imprisoned in Wormwood Scrubs after trying to print a collection of his poems entitled *Here Lies John Penis*. In 1932, Count Potocki , who, despite the inconvenient fact that he had been born in Auckland, New Zealand, claimed to be the rightful King of Poland, took a selection of his poems and translations to a printer and asked him to produce 50 copies for distribution among his friends. Unfortunately, the man he chose was also the printer of the *Methodist Recorder* and he decided that the poems were obscene. He informed the authorities and Montalk was sent for trial. Not helping his cause by arriving at court dressed in a red robe and sandals, Montalk received a six-month prison sentence. 'A man must not say he is a poet and be filthy,' the magistrate remarked in passing judgement.

Of the long-established nightclubs, the Gargoyle was still thriving. Not as fashionable as it had been in the twenties, it still attracted a diverse clientele. The short-story writer William Sansom remembered it as 'full of literary people and drunken dukes'. Drunken actors could also be found there. Robert Newton, fresh from his triumph as Long John Silver in the Disney film of *Treasure Island*, once stripped off his clothes and took to the small stage, there to do an impression of the peg-legged pirate taking a dip in the briny. Still naked, the well-oiled Newton returned to his seat and promptly fell asleep. A passing waiter stuck a lit cigar in his mouth as other members applauded the performance. On another occasion, Lucian Freud, artist and grandson of the famous Sigmund, was sitting in the club minding his own business when he was hauled to his feet and punched in the jaw by a fellow member. 'There's one for you,' his assailant shouted and, while the dazed Freud was still recovering, he punched him again. 'And there's one for your beastly old grandfather!'

Then there were the afternoon drinking clubs in which, after time had been called in the pubs, further hours could be agreeably wasted in booze, backbiting and gossip. The most famous of these was the Colony Room in Dean Street, run by the formidable Muriel Belcher. Born in Birmingham in 1908, Belcher came from a well-off Jewish family which had owned a theatre in that city. Moving to London in the thirties, she had established a theatrical and society club called the Music Box in Leicester Place, which was open throughout the war. Her new venture opened its doors in December 1948. Just a few weeks later, Francis Bacon made his first visit there, in company with Brian Howard. He and Muriel Belcher hit it off so well and so immediately that she suggested he should act as a kind of recruiting agent for the club, bringing in those people he knew and liked. In return she would let him drink for free and pay him £10 a week. Throughout the fifties, sixties and seventies, the Colony Room became the favoured Soho retreat for those who preferred to spend their afternoons drinking rather than working. Regulars ranged from poets like Dylan Thomas and Louis MacNeice to artists and friends of Francis Bacon such as Lucian Freud, Frank Auerbach and John Minton. However, there was never any doubting who was the Queen of the Colony. Perched on her high stool at the bar, near to the entrance so that she could monitor new arrivals and, if need be, tell them to 'fuck

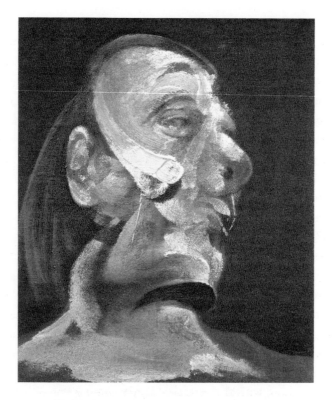

STUDY OF MURIEL BELCHER, FRANCIS BACON, 1966

off', Muriel Belcher was a spectacularly rude and foul-mouthed, but often witty, hostess. Her favourite term of endearment was 'cunty'. Camper than Christmas, she called most men 'she' or 'Mrs' and, as one regular has remarked, 'it could be disconcerting when some elderly major was introduced with the words, "She was a very gallant little lady on the Somme".' It was arguably even more disconcerting when she reminisced about the Blitz and called it 'the time when we were all fighting that nasty Mrs Hitler'.

Not everyone found the Colony Room to their taste. The Liverpool poet Brian Patten called it 'a small urinal full of fractious old geezers bitching about each other'. To those who did like it, it was unmatchable. The dishevelled poet and Soho habitué Paul Potts summed up its appeal under Muriel Belcher's aegis as well as anyone. 'The relatively small room which is her domain and where she is an absolute sovereign must be one of the most unique rooms anywhere,' he wrote in a letter. 'It is the sort of place where you can't get much for ten bob but you can get an awful lot for nothing. Once you're in, you're in; the poor and the private get treated just as well as the rich and famous. But if she doesn't like you – you've had it.' There is a painting of the Colony Room by Michael Andrews, now in the Pallant House Gallery in Chichester, which neatly depicts its dark and smoky appeal and shows regulars, including Bruce and Jeffrey Bernard, Henrietta Moraes, Francis Bacon and Muriel Belcher herself, packed into its narrow confines. Belcher died in 1979 and the Colony Room was taken over by her barman Ian Board (known as 'Ida'), who was, if anything, even ruder than she was. Despite Board's habit of losing track of where he'd stashed the takings when drunk, the club continued to thrive. After his death it was run by his long-time barman Michael Wojas, who gained a new clientele, as the old one died off, with the arrival of hard-drinking Young British Artists like Damien Hirst and Tracey Emin and Britpop musicians like Alex James. After bickering and acrimony between Wojas and club members, the Colony Room finally closed its doors at the end of 2008.

The Caves de France was also in Dean Street. According to the novelist Elaine Dundy, first wife of Kenneth Tynan, the Caves was 'a sort of coal-hole in the heart of Soho that is open every afternoon, a dead-ended subterranean tunnel', possessed of an 'atmosphere almost solid with failure'. Others described it with greater fondness. To the writer and early TV personality Dan Farson, with its 'rich assortment of eccentrics and veteran drinkers, young and old and mostly poor', it was 'true bohemia'. The barman in the Caves was Secundo Primera, brother of

Primo Carnera, the so-called Ambling Alp who had been world heavyweight boxing champion in the 1930s. Their mother, short on inspiration, had simply numbered her sons rather than naming them. Regulars included the two Roberts, Caitlin Thomas, Nina Hamnett, Elizabeth Smart and the shambolic poet Paul Potts. Occasional visitors included the deeply sinister and then ageing Gerald Hamilton, allegedly the model for the title character in Christopher Isherwood's novel *Mr Norris Changes Trains*. At various times in his life, Hamilton was a Communist, a pacifist, a Nazi sympathiser, an apologist for apartheid and a flatmate of the 'Great Beast', Aleister Crowley. He was the only Englishman to be arrested for treason in both World Wars. In the First World War, he was imprisoned for aiding Irish nationalists. During the Second World War, he decided that he should embark on his own unilateral peace talks with Germany, where he had lived for much of the thirties, and was intending to travel to neutral Ireland to begin the process, but was refused an exit visa from Britain. When he tried to flee the country disguised as a nun, he was detained and sent to Brixton Prison. In the 1950s, at about the time he was frequenting the Caves, he posed for the sculptor Oscar Nemon, who had been commissioned to create a statue of Winston Churchill. Since Churchill was too busy to sit for him, Nemon enlisted the help of Hamilton, who was much the same size and build as the wartime leader. Perhaps unsurprisingly, Churchill was furious when the story leaked to the newspapers that a man twice interned for treason had been his body double.

The Mandrake Club in Meard Street was opened just after the war, initially as a chess club, by Teddy Turner and Boris Watson, a Bulgarian who had begun life with the more obviously Slavic name of Boris Protopopov. As early as 1953 it was advertising itself as 'London's only bohemian rendezvous' and the likes of Nina Hamnett, Julian Maclaren-Ross and Brian Howard were familiar faces at its bar. Because the licensing laws stipulated that alcohol could only be served with food, the club offered sandwiches for sale, most of them tired and elderly. If anyone complained they were inedible, the proprietor could be heard saying, with weary patience, 'This is a sandwich for drinking with, not eating'. The Horseshoe Club in Wardour Street was a regular haunt for Dylan Thomas, who loved the sliding panel on its door, enabling people inside to see who was outside, because it conjured up images of a Prohibition-era speakeasy in Chicago. Other rendezvous for the Soho pleasure-seeker included the Moonglow Club in Percy Street, the Byron in Greek Street, the Club Côte d'Azur ('Un Coin de Provence à Londres', as it optimistically called itself), the Little Sweden Club, Miranda's Club, and the Gay Compton Club.

Almost a kind of club and certainly an important locus for 1950s and early 1960s bohemia was David Archer's bookshop in Greek Street, which opened in 1956. Archer had inherited money from a rich father and spent several decades impoverishing himself by handing it out to a succession of needy writers, as well as to the sailors with whom he slept. 'He owned a third of Wiltshire and could not wait to give it away,' as the playwright Bernard Kops once remarked. Before the war, he had run an earlier incarnation of his bookshop and had published volumes of poetry by the likes of Dylan Thomas, George Barker and the teenage English surrealist David Gascoyne. Although, in one sense, Archer was not a very good bookseller – he seemed actively averse to selling his books and would often recommend customers to go elsewhere to buy them – his Greek Street shop became a kind of downmarket literary salon for the young writers of the period. Regulars ranged from Colin MacInnes and Colin Wilson to poets such as Dom Moraes, Christopher Logue and Robert Nye. By the sixties, Archer had given nearly all his money away. He worked briefly in the lampshade department of Selfridges and ended up taking an overdose of aspirin in a hostel for the homeless in Stepney in 1971.

Francis and Friends

If anyone was king of this fifties Soho of pubs and drinking clubs, it was the painter Francis Bacon. Born in Dublin in 1909, Bacon came from a comfortably off, upper middle-class family. His father was a retired army officer and racehorse trainer, his mother an heiress to a fortune made in stainless steel. Ejected from the family home at the age of 17, after his father found him posing in front of a mirror while dressed in his mother's underwear, Bacon embarked on a peripatetic career in London, Berlin and Paris. He worked intermittently as an interior decorator and, during the war, he ran an illegal casino in his rooms and studio opposite the Natural History Museum. In 1945, his triptych *Three Studies for Figures at the Base of a Crucifixion*, painted the previous year, established his reputation as one of the most exciting and original talents in British art. It was one that he never lost during the remaining decades of his life. He also gained a reputation as a *bon vivant* and bohemian. A party at Bacon's studio in 1950, held to celebrate the marriage of his friend Michael Wishart and the painter Ann Dunn, lasted two days and three nights and was described by David Tennant, owner of the Gargoyle Club, as 'the first real party since the war'. Bacon painted the chandeliers in his studio crimson and welcomed 200 guests, including Muriel Belcher, Graham Sutherland and Ann Dunn's maid of honour, a chanteuse known as 'the bugger's Vera Lynn', because she had run a drinking club during the war which catered largely for gay servicemen. The decade that followed was Bacon's heyday as a boozy barfly. He once described his everyday life as 'going from bar to bar and drinking and that sort of thing', although, unlike many of the courtiers who accompanied him as he processed unsteadily around Soho, he made sure that he had put in plenty of hours of work before heading for the French House or the Colony Room.

UNFINISHED PORTRAIT OF FRANCIS BACON BY LUCIAN FREUD, 1956-1957

One of Bacon's closest friends and associates was the photographer John Deakin. Described by George Melly as 'a vicious little drunk of such inventive malice and implacable bitchiness that it's surprising he didn't choke on his own venom', Deakin had been born in the Wirral in 1912. He had begun his working life as a painter, but turned to photography in the late thirties. In the forties and fifties he worked for *Vogue*. He was sacked from the magazine not once, but twice, because his drinking made him unreliable and because he had an alarming propensity for mislaying valuable photographic equipment when under the influence. His best work was as a portrait photographer and some of the defining images of fifties Soho bohemia (John Minton with his head in his hands, a young Jeffrey Bernard looking improbably handsome in Cambridge Circus and Francis Bacon holding aloft two huge joints of meat) are his. Deakin's first major exhibitions of his photographs were in 1956 at the Greek Street bookshop and gallery owned by his sometime lover David Archer, but, despite critical acclaim, he was notoriously dismissive of photography as an art form. It may well be that he still yearned to be acknowledged, like his friend Bacon, as a painter.

Dan Farson has a memorable description of meeting Deakin for the first time in the French House. He was 'curiously dishevelled as if he had been rescued at sea and fitted out in clothes donated by the crew: paint-smeared blue jeans whose zip was half-open, and a thick white polo-neck sweater now grey with age, on which blood had fallen from the ridge of congealed gore behind his ear. On top he wore his version of a British officer's "warm", a tattered sheepskin overcoat which was a graveyard of nostalgic wine stains and cigarette burns as if he had fallen asleep in it on countless nights... I was entranced.' Farson also tells a later story of Deakin, Francis Bacon and himself drinking in a basement gay club called the Rockingham. Deakin passed out and had to be carried up the stairs and out of the premises amidst the queenly tut-tutting of other drinkers. Bacon paused at the top of the stairs and shouted down, 'Even unconscious, he's more fun than you lot!' Deakin died in Brighton of a heart attack in 1972. He had named Bacon as his next of kin and the painter was obliged to identify the body. 'It was the last dirty trick he played on me,' Bacon said. 'They lifted up the sheet,' he went on, 'and there he was, his trap shut for the first time in his life.' After his death, his friend and fellow photographer Bruce Bernard, older brother of Jeffrey, visited Deakin's flat in Berwick Street and found a large collection of his photos stuffed under the bed, many of them the images by which he is best known today.

Other painters shared the same Soho territory as Bacon. Lucian Freud was born in Berlin in 1922, the grandson of Sigmund Freud, founder of psychoanalysis, and moved with his family to London when the Nazis came to power in Germany. After periods in Paris and Dublin as a young artist, he settled in the city in the fifties and became a familiar face in the pubs and clubs of Soho. Married twice (to Kitty Garman, daughter of Jacob Epstein and Kathleen Garman, and to Lady Caroline Blackwood) and divorced twice, Freud was notorious as a womaniser. He was also renowned as a reckless gambler. 'Debt stimulates me,' he once said and he borrowed wildly and unwisely to fund his fondness for the horses. On one occasion he confessed to a friend that he had borrowed from the Kray twins and they were threatening to cut off his hand if he didn't pay them back. On another, he was walking with fellow painter Tim Behrens when a man approached them and said, 'Hello, Lou, how funny seeing you'. Instead of replying, Freud immediately headbutted the man and, shouting 'Run!' to Behrens, legged it down the street. When they were both at a safe distance, Freud acknowledged that the man was a gangster and he owed him £14,000. Like Bacon, Freud went on to become one of twentieth-century Britain's most critically and commercially successful artists.

A less familiar name today is that of John Minton. Minton came from a wealthy family with connections to the Minton ceramics factory. He studied at St John's Wood School of Art in the 1930s, before travelling abroad with fellow student Michael Ayrton. In 1943, he moved into a shared studio in Bedford Gardens with the two Roberts, Colquhoun and MacBryde, which rapidly became notorious as a boozy open house for other artists. By the 1950s, having long since left the two Roberts behind and moved into his own house in Kensington, Minton was one of the best-known artists in London, as likely to appear in the gossip columns of the newspapers as in their review pages. His taste for Soho nightlife attracted attention, but did little to offset his underlying melancholy, so brilliantly captured in Deakin's photo of him and in a portrait by Lucian Freud. A regular at the Gargoyle, where Ruthven Todd once witnessed him dancing 'a frenetic solo on the otherwise unoccupied dance floor', Minton was also a familiar face at the other well-known clubs, often surrounded by an entourage of off-duty sailors eager to down the drinks he generously bought them. By the second half of the decade, his reputation was in decline and his personal problems were exacerbated by his increasing dependence on drink. On 20 January 1957, still 11 months short of his fortieth birthday, he committed suicide.

One of Minton's closest friends was Henrietta Moraes, the muse of 1950s Soho. Born Audrey Wendy Abbott in Simla, India in 1931, she was educated in a series of convent schools and then plunged into London nightlife and Soho bohemia as a young model for painters like Lucian Freud and, via revealing photos taken of her by John Deakin, Francis Bacon. In later life, she reported that Deakin had turned up at her flat with his camera and 'told me to lie on the bed with my legs open. And he began taking photos from the wrong end. I said, "Deakin, I don't think that's what Francis wants. I don't think that would interest him." "Oh no," said Deakin, "this is the way Francis wants it." But of course he didn't, so we had to start all over again.' Later, she discovered that Deakin was selling copies of the first set of photos to porn shops in Soho at ten shillings a time. Unsurprisingly, she described the photographer as 'a horrible little man'.

For a time, Moraes ran the coffee shop in David Archer's bookshop in Greek Street, where 'she discharged her duties with a sort of ferocious efficiency, and was constantly surrounded with young writers, with whom she carried on bantering flirtations'. She was possessed of a sexual assertiveness and lack of inhibition that young women were not supposed to display so openly in the 1950s, as her own account of the beginning of her relationship with Freud demonstrates. 'I was dancing with Lucian in the Gargoyle one night,' she wrote, 'and said to him, "I want you." We made a date to meet at lunchtime the next day in a basement off Brewer Street and there consummated, on the edge of an unwieldy kitchen sink, our friendship.' John Minton, a gay man with whom she developed an intense, but platonic relationship, left her his house when he killed himself in 1957. Within a few years, however, her life, never very orderly, began to descend into chaos. 'I picked up bad habits like a magnet does iron filings,' she later wrote. Her marriage to the young poet Dom Moraes brought her a new name, but little in the way of happiness; she drank too much and became addicted to amphetamines, attempting suicide on several occasions. In the sixties, she became a pioneering hippy, living in a gypsy caravan in a West Country commune, and had a brief, unsuccessful career as a cat burglar which landed her in Holloway Prison. In later life, she sobered up and published a revealing memoir entitled simply *Henrietta*. At the time of her death in 1999, she was planning another volume, to be called either *Encore Henrietta*, or, more eye-catchingly, *Fuck Off, Darling*, her signature remark from her heyday as Queen of bohemian Soho.

Over the years, the most assiduous chronicler of those Soho days was Dan Farson. He was the son of Negley Farson, an American reporter and adventurous foreign correspondent who had written an autobiographical volume called *The Way of the Transgressor*, which had become an unexpected bestseller in the 1930s. His mother was the niece of Bram Stoker, creator of Dracula. Farson Jr, who had once been patted on the head and described by Hitler as 'a good Aryan boy' during one of his father's visits to Nazi Germany, grew up to be an early star of commercial broadcasting in the UK. *Out of Step*, first shown in 1957, was a series of documentaries, fronted by Farson, in which he went in search of people (nudists, scientologists, white witches) with unconventional opinions. He first arrived in Soho in the early fifties when, in his own words, 'London was suffering from post-war depression and it was a revelation to discover people who behaved outrageously without a twinge of guilt and drank so recklessly that when they met next morning they had to ask if they needed to apologise for the night before.' In later life, and in books like *Soho in the Fifties*, he memorialised the bohemia in which he was happiest. He moved away from London to live in Devon, but regularly returned to old Soho haunts where he was a familiar figure, renowned for his Jekyll and Hyde transformations under the influence of drink. All charm when sober ('Dear boy, how nice to see you. How are you?'), he often became recklessly offensive as the evening progressed, spitting verbal venom at his victims and wishing them early and painful deaths.

It is all too easy to view the Soho of the 1950s through retrospectively rose-tinted glasses and Dan Farson's works are among those many books written about the period which have conspired to create the illusion of a happy oasis of creativity and nonconformity in a dull and conventional London. For those who lived through the era (and not everybody survived), it was not always so simple. In the words of Norman Bowler, the actor who was Henrietta Moraes's second husband, 'Soho was a very painful place to be. People weren't getting drunk and abusing each other out of fun. It was pain.' The last voice representing this classic Soho bohemia was probably that of Jeffrey Bernard. Bernard, the son of an architect and an opera singer, was first seduced by the louche glamour of the area as a schoolboy in the late 1940s. He was a regular in its pubs and drinking clubs throughout its 1950s and 1960s heyday when Francis Bacon held court in the Colony Room and the likes of Deakin, Farson and the two Roberts staggered through its streets. As the decades passed, the artists and writers began to disappear, succumbing to the varying demands of drink, fame and domesticity. Like a dutiful soldier, doggedly sticking to his post when others had deserted, Bernard stayed in Soho. By the eighties and nineties, as Hugh David and others have remarked, the district had become a kind of 'theme park', in which yuppies could play at being bohemian by visiting the Coach and Horses in Greek Street and watching Bernard drink himself literally legless.

(After losing a leg as a consequence of his lifestyle, Bernard allegedly put a personal ad in *The Spectator* which read, 'Alcoholic, diabetic amputee seeks sympathy fuck'. Some years earlier he had been invited by a publisher to write his autobiography and had similarly chosen to resort to the personal ads of *The Spectator*. He placed one in which he asked if anyone could remember what he was doing between 1960 and 1974.) In 1989, he became (briefly) more famous when Keith Waterhouse's play *Jeffrey Bernard is Unwell* opened in the West End and audiences could watch Peter O'Toole's impersonation of him. In Waterhouse's words, Bernard was the 'Huckleberry Finn of Soho. The rest of us were going home and paying mortgages and educating children, but Jeff was paddling his raft up and down Old Compton Street.' It was not an easy life. As Iain Sinclair once wrote, 'Late-bohemianism is a career better recollected than experienced.' When Bernard died in 1997, one part of London's bohemian history died with him.

Outsiders and Angry Young Men

Side by side with what might be termed the traditional bohemia experienced and later recorded by Dan Farson, there was a new cultural phenomenon, partly genuine, but mostly generated by the media, which came up with the title of 'Angry Young Men'. Such disparate talents as John Osborne, Kingsley Amis and John Braine were all clubbed together in a literary movement that had little reality outside the pages of the press. Some of its supposed members had never even met one another. The archetypal Angry Young Man, at least as imagined by the newspapers, was Colin Wilson. Born in Leicester, the son of a factory worker, Wilson decided he was a genius when he was a teenager. 'I hadn't the faintest doubt of my genius,' he told a later interviewer, 'and I could see no good reason why I shouldn't become either the greatest writer or greatest scientist the world has ever known. Sometimes a feeling of my talent so overwhelmed me that it gave me a headache.' He rarely wavered in this belief in his own brilliance, despite mounting evidence to the contrary, until his death in 2013. After avoiding National Service by claiming (falsely) to be gay, he arrived in London in the mid-fifties. Sleeping rough at nights in a sleeping bag on Hampstead Heath, in order to save money, he spent his days writing in the British Museum Reading Room. In 1956, he became famous as the author of *The Outsider*, a rambling, idiosyncratic study of the artist as exile from conventional society, which was acclaimed as a masterpiece by an array of critics who ought to have known better. Wilson was hailed by the media as both an 'Angry Young Man' and as a bohemian of a more old-fashioned and immediately recognisable kind. Cast out of the harmless obscurity of his Hampstead Heath sleeping bag, he was suddenly thrust into the spotlight and this was not always a comfortable place to be. His private life was subject to ruthless scrutiny, culminating in a bizarre confrontation with his future father-in-law, which was gleefully recorded by the newspapers.

Wilson had been living in Notting Hill with a girlfriend, Joy Stewart. Her father had come across some notes for a novel Wilson was planning about a sex murderer and assumed that they were a diary. Eager to rescue his daughter from the clutches of an obvious fiend, the father burst into a party Wilson was giving. Armed with a horsewhip and reportedly shouting, 'You're a homosexual with six mistresses,' Mr Stewart faced up to the author, who promptly burst into hysterical laughter. The story made it into the papers just as the critics who had so hailed him for *The Outsider* were beginning to revise their opinions downwards. Wilson retreated to Cornwall where he lived for the next 50 years, nursing his self-proclaimed genius and writing dozens of books on subjects ranging from Atlantis and alien abductions to serial killers and the occult.

His literary reputation, briefly so high, has long since dissipated, but his 1961 novel, *Adrift in Soho*, still provides a fascinating portrait

COLIN WILSON AND JOY STEWART IN THEIR NOTTING HILL FLAT, 1957

of Soho and Notting Hill in the fifties. It follows the fortunes of its teenage narrator Harry Preston, a silly and pretentious, but somehow endearing, autodidact who is clearly a version of Wilson himself. Arriving in London in flight from the dullness of his provincial town, Harry falls in with a succession of Soho characters, who educate him in the manners and mores of the city while he tries to write his philosophical masterpiece about the nature of freedom. After a series of misadventures, he ends up living with his recently acquired New Zealand girlfriend in a Notting Hill house-cum-commune populated largely by mad artists and their nubile, submissive models.

Adrift in Soho is not a very good novel, but Wilson was working in a recognisable tradition of fiction about young men struggling to assert themselves in London's bohemia. An earlier and much better post-war example is *Scamp*, first published by John Lehmann

ROLAND CAMBERTON'S *SCAMP*, 1950

in 1950 with a dust jacket designed by John Minton. It won the 1951 Somerset Maugham Award. Written by the mysterious, pseudonymous Roland Camberton, who disappeared from view later in the decade, it is the story of Ginsberg, a 31-year-old habitué of the seedier pubs and clubs of Soho and Bloomsbury, who decides to launch a literary magazine. An assortment of chance encounters, misunderstandings and odd adventures ensues. Camberton's novel includes thinly disguised portraits of a number of familiar figures from the bohemia of the immediate post-war years, perhaps most notably Julian Maclaren-Ross, who appears as Angus Sternforth Simms, a writer holding forth to a gang of cronies in a Soho pub. The portrait is sufficiently biting that it comes as no surprise that Maclaren-Ross, reviewing Camberton's novel when it was first published, stated that the author 'appears to be devoid of any narrative gift'. Reading *Scamp* today, it's possible to see what Maclaren-Ross meant, although the book is lively and often funny. It deserves a wider readership than it has ever had.

However, the most vivid and vital of all the Soho novels of the fifties is probably *Absolute Beginners*, published two years before Wilson's book, and written by Colin MacInnes, another regular in Soho's pubs and clubs in the fifties. The son of the popular novelist Angela Thirkell, and distantly related to both Rudyard Kipling and the Conservative Prime Minister Stanley Baldwin, MacInnes fiercely rejected the world in which he grew up. He was gay when the expression of gay sexuality was still illegal and an eccentric champion of radical causes. Arrogant and irascible (George Melly called him 'one of the great quarrellers of our time'), he was also the first significant white writer to look sympathetically at the black culture that was emerging in post-war London. His interest in it was largely shaped by his sexual attraction to young black men, but it was genuine. (The playwright Bernard Kops recalled meeting MacInnes in the Colony Room where he was sucking on a passion fruit, an exotic foodstuff in 1950s London. Kops remarked on how wrinkled the strange fruit was. 'Just like a black boy's balls,' MacInnes replied.) His debut novel *City of Spades*, published in 1957, is one of the first books to explore the racial issues facing some areas of London. *Absolute Beginners* examines another social phenomenon of the time – the rise of the teenager. The unnamed teenage narrator of the novel was based on a young man named Terry Taylor. MacInnes had met Taylor when the latter was working as a passport photographer in Wardour Street and introduced him to Ida Kar, an old-style continental bohemian, originally from Russia, who ran Gallery One in D'Arblay Street with her husband Victor Musgrave. Taylor became Kar's assistant and later lover, despite a 25-year age difference. (Taylor himself later published a novel, *Baron's Court, All Change*, which is well worth reading.) *Absolute Beginners* remains an exceptionally vivid evocation of 1950s Soho where, as the narrator says, 'all the things they say happen, do; I mean the vice of every kink', and of Notting Hill, scene of the race riots which form the backdrop to the novel's climactic scenes.

The differences between *Absolute Beginners* and the novels by Camberton and Wilson are worth highlighting. The anti-heroes of *Scamp* and *Adrift in Soho* are out to make their names in literature; the narrator of MacInnes's book is a photographer. (Photography was to become both one of the sexier arts of the sixties and a ladder for talented working-class young men to climb, as witnessed by the careers of David Bailey and Terence Donovan.) The supporting cast of characters in *Scamp* and *Adrift in Soho* are painters, philosophers and traditional bohemian eccentrics; in *Absolute Beginners* the narrator's friends are mostly teenagers, obsessed by clothes and jazz. Roland Camberton and Colin Wilson are looking back to past paradigms of London bohemia; MacInnes is glimpsing a future in which literature and the visual arts will lose their primacy and music will take centre stage. Two years before *Absolute Beginners* was published, Guy Deghy and Keith Waterhouse wrote in a history of the Café Royal that, 'Bohemianism is obviously finished. There may be some isolated cases – the odd chap in the attic – but on the whole much of the struggle has been removed from the artistic career.' In one sense, they were clearly wrong. Traditional English bohemianism was actually reaching an apogee at the time they were writing its obituary. In another sense, just as MacInnes was to do, they had hit upon some underlying truth about the changing nature of bohemianism. The days of eccentric poets in the Café Royal and boozy artists in the Caves de France were numbered. Bohemianism still had a future, but it was to lie in different locales.

Chapter Eight

WORKING-CLASS BOHEMIA

From Trad Jazz to Rock 'n' Roll

THROUGHOUT ITS HISTORY, bohemia had been almost exclusively a home for renegade and maverick members of the upper and middle classes. This all began to change in the fifties. As the art critic Kenneth Coutts-Smith noted, 'The Fifties saw a social phenomenon that had never previously existed at any moment of the past, the appearance of a working-class bohemia. The Teds were the vanguard, the first thin wedge of an emergent social group that was soon to count within the body politic.' This new bohemia was inextricably intertwined with new kinds of music.

The musical revolution had begun before the war with jazz. There had been plenty of jazz clubs in 1930s Soho. The Shim Sham on Wardour Street, opened in 1935, was perhaps the most famous of these. Regularly described as 'London's Cotton Club', it was a place where the city's black musicians could play and mingle with a heterogeneous audience of Sohoites, celebrities, gays, gangsters and members of 'high bohemia'. Although it was regularly hailed as an example of the city's growing cosmopolitanism, the Shim Sham also attracted the attention of the law. A series of anonymous letters condemned the club ('the encouragement of Black and White intercourse is the talk of the town', one declared) and stirred the police into action. Undercover officers descended on the Shim Sham in search of evidence and its owner, Jack Isow, was soon charged with running an unlicensed club and fined. Undeterred by the court case and by continued police surveillance, Isow kept the Shim Sham going for a couple of years and had several more run-ins with the authorities during a club-owning career that lasted into the 1950s. The Shim Sham itself closed at the end of 1937.

After a period of hibernation during the war, London's jazz scene was reinvigorated in the late 1940s and early 1950s. New clubs were established. Club Eleven opened in Ham Yard, Great Windmill Street in 1948 and soon had two house bands, one led by Ronnie Scott and one by John Dankworth. In the following decade it metamorphosed into Cy Laurie's Jazz Club, famous for its 'All-nite Rave-ups', which went on to 6am when the tube started running again. 'We used to take dexadrine or benzedrine,' one regular at the club remembered, 'feel really great and stay up all night, jiving and smooching. It was licensed anarchy. And all the time, there'd be someone reading Sartre in the corner. About six in the morning you'd go out into the street, find a caff and have breakfast with all the prostitutes, who were just knocking off.' It all sounds fairly innocuous today, but, in the 1950s, this was living on the edge. By the end of the decade, even more jazz clubs – like the legendary Ronnie Scott's, established in a basement in Gerrard Street – had opened. There were also clubs dedicated to newer kinds of music. The Gyre and Gimble in John Adam Street was given over to skiffle and, as writer Barry Miles has noted, 'Skiffle introduced a younger crowd to the London bohemian mix.'

A newer phenomenon than the old-fashioned drinking clubs and jazz clubs was the arrival in Soho of Italian-style coffee bars. Coffee houses had, of course, existed in London for centuries. The

first one, run by a former manservant from Turkey named Pasqua
Rosee, had opened in St Michael's Alley, Cornhill in 1652. The
long tradition of the coffee house as intellectual rendezvous and
talking shop was carried on in 1950s Soho. The Nucleus Coffee
House in Monmouth Street was open in the early hours of the
morning to members who paid five shillings a year and was a
favourite haunt of musicians, eccentrics and insomniacs. The
House of Sam Widges in D'Arblay Street was run by the musician,
painter and later playwright Neil Oram and, according to one
visitor, was 'filled with itinerant poets, nursing cups of cold coffee'.
More overtly political was the Partisan in Carlisle Street, located
in rooms below the Left Book Club, which was a meeting place
for CND activists and other radicals. These 1950s coffee bars were
different to old-fashioned cafés and coffee houses. Some were
aggressively modern in their formica and stainless steel fittings,
others more eccentric in decoration. The Heaven and Hell had
two floors, an upstairs painted white to represent heaven and a
black basement where a skiffle group called The Ghouls regularly
played. Le Macabre in Meard Street lived up to its name by using
coffins as tables and Bakelite skulls as ashtrays.

The most famous of the coffee bars was soon the 2i's in Old
Compton Street, named after its original owners Freddie and
Sammy Irani, in which British rock 'n' roll had its beginnings in
1956 and 1957. The 2i's became a recruiting centre for the first
generation of London rockers after it was taken over by Paul
Lincoln, an Australian wrestler known as 'Dr Death', and his
business partner Ray Hunter. Tommy Hicks, soon to be dubbed
Tommy Steele, was discovered by photographer and would-be
impresario John Kennedy while performing there and was signed
up by Decca. When Steele rapidly gained nationwide fame and
the story of his discovery became widely known, the coffee bar
found itself the epicentre of the new music. 'If it was good enough
for Tommy Steele,' future Shadows guitarist Bruce Welch noted

years later, 'it was good enough for us' and went on to recall the atmosphere in the 2i's. 'It was a small place, very hot and very sweaty, with a tiny eighteen-inch high stage at one end, a microphone and a few old speakers up on the wall. It wasn't exactly salubrious, but it was always packed. Other people would come up to us and say, Can I sit in? And they'd get up and play with us. It was like a big jam session. All these would-be musicians dreaming of being rock-stars.' Cliff Richard, Adam Faith and Joe Brown were all amongst the hopefuls who played there in the late fifties. This was also the era of beat Svengali Larry Parnes, dubbed 'Mr Parnes, Shillings and Pence' by the press, who joined with John Kennedy in managing Tommy Steele and groomed a series of handsome young men for pop stardom. Parnes changed their often mundane names to something more eye-catching and launched them in the direction of the charts. Ron Wycherley became Billy Fury, Roy Taylor was rechristened Vince Eager and Reg Patterson became Marty Wilde. (Joe Brown wisely resisted Parnes's attempts to rename him Elmer Twitch.) British rock and roll stuttered into life in the coffee bars of Old Compton Street and a new decade was on the horizon.

The Swinging Sixties Dawn

By the time that new decade dawned, some were already mourning the death of Soho. In 1961 Colin MacInnes wrote that 'Soho is dead, except commercially. Soho, at one time, owed its reputation to its people: now the area bestows a bogus reputation on almost anything.' MacInnes was, of course, premature in his obituary. The afternoon drinking clubs still survived. Muriel Belcher still ruled the roost at the Colony Room. The Kismet Club on Great Newport Street, 'a subterranean charnel smokehouse' as it has been described, remained 'notorious for its smell of old snout and mildew'. 'What's that smell?' a neophyte visitor to the Kismet is supposed to have once asked. 'Failure', a regular instantly replied. However, the world of London's bohemia was undoubtedly changing. The driving force was no longer poetry or the visual arts. It was popular music. The new bohemians were not poets in garrets or artists in cramped and draughty studios, but musicians strumming guitars in seedy flats. Today, when they are multi-millionaires with all the trappings of excessive wealth, it's easy to forget that Mick Jagger and Keith Richards, for example, began their careers as escapees from their lower middle-class backgrounds, living in squalor in two rooms of a house in Edith Grove, SW10.

Soho still had its role to play in this changing bohemia. 'British rock 'n' roll,' according to Barry Miles, 'was born in a handful of small clubs in the early sixties.' Many of these were in Soho. Nearly all of them had begun as jazz clubs, then metamorphosed into different venues with the arrival of new forms of music. The Flamingo in Wardour Street, which had opened in the previous decade, became a mecca for the burgeoning number of British fans of American R & B. Musician Georgie Fame, who had a three-year residency there, remembered it as a place where 'only a handful of hip young white people' used to go. Half the clientele in the early sixties were West Indian and the other half, according to Fame, 'were black American GIs mixed up with a few gangsters and pimps and prostitutes'. In October 1962, the club was the scene of a knife fight between 'Lucky' Gordon, brother of one of Fame's backing band, and a man named Johnny Edgecombe. Both men were lovers of model and dancer Christine Keeler and their fight, which ended with unlucky Lucky needing 17 stitches to a wound in his face, was the starting point for a long sequence of events which eventually led to revelations about Keeler's other affairs, including compromising ones with British cabinet minister John Profumo and Soviet diplomat and spy Yevgeny Ivanov. By the middle of the decade the Flamingo's fame had spread far beyond the ranks of R & B cognoscenti and it had become the haunt of British pop aristocracy, from Paul McCartney to Brian Jones.

GEORGIE FAME AT THE FLAMINGO CLUB, SOHO, LONDON, 1964

Other gathering places for a new generation included the Scene Club in Ham Yard off Windmill Street, stamping ground for mods, the Ad Lib in Leicester Place and La Discotheque in Wardour Street, the first place in London to play only recorded music to its audiences. The 100 Club on Oxford Street began life as the Feldman Swing Club in 1942, where Glenn Miller visited and black musicians from America and the empire were welcomed. During the fifties it was briefly the home of Humphrey Lyttelton's jazz band. It became the 100 Club in 1964 and nearly all the major bands of the sixties played there. Perhaps the most famous of all the clubs was the Marquee, which began as a jazz and skiffle venue in Oxford Street in the late fifties, but had its golden era during the sixties after it had moved to Wardour Street. Scene of the Rolling Stones' first gig in July 1962, the Marquee played host to many other now legendary bands in their early days, including

The Yardbirds, Manfred Mann, The Who and The Moody Blues. It was also the venue, in spring 1966, for the 'Spontaneous Underground' happenings, where poets, performance artists and experimental groups, including Pink Floyd, joined forces to celebrate a new energy in all the arts.

Old and new generations of bohemia had earlier come together at the First International Poetry Incarnation in the Royal Albert Hall on 11 June 1965. Originating with the idea of a poetry reading for Allen Ginsberg and other beat poets when they visited London, this escalated into a major event. Michael Horovitz, one of the organisers, recalled the writing of a manifesto: 'We sat in Alex Trocchi's sordid flat – there were heroin needles on the floor – and took it in turns to speak lines that Ginsberg wrote down. That formed our manifesto.' Nobody knew whether anyone would actually come to the Albert Hall, which was booked in a fit of hubris when someone mentioned that it was the largest venue in London, but in the end all 8,000 tickets were sold. The event was introduced by Trocchi, a heroin-addicted veteran of bohemian communities around the world, from Paris (where he had earned a living writing pornography for legendary publisher Maurice Girodias) to California. Trocchi was praised for his aplomb in compèring what was potentially an explosive mix of egos and temperaments, although as one writer has pointed out, since he 'was taking twenty grains of heroin and seven of cocaine per day, it certainly took a lot to faze him'. One of his plans for publicising the event had been to sacrifice a chicken on an altar in the middle of the reading, but he had been reluctantly persuaded that this might attract unnecessary attention from the police.

Both performers and audience at the Albert Hall that day were a mixed crew, although it is noticeable, in retrospect, that all the poets who read were white and male. Ginsberg himself was drunk and, at one point while reciting his own poems, announced, 'I want God to fuck me up the ass.' According to poet and playwright

Heathcote Williams, present in the audience, an angry man in a bowler hat, who had clearly misjudged the nature of the event he was attending, then shouted out, 'We want poetry! This is not poetry!' Ginsberg turned to him and shouted in reply, 'I want *you* to fuck me up the ass!' Ginsberg's fellow American beats Gregory Corso and Lawrence Ferlinghetti gave very different readings. Corso, sitting down with his back to half the audience, could hardly be heard as he recited lengthy verses he had only recently completed. Ferlinghetti roared out one of his own poems entitled 'To Fuck is to Love Again', which helped to shock not only the more easily shockable members of the audience, but also a number of British Legion members who were working as attendants at the event. London protest poet Adrian Mitchell became the surprise star of the show with his reading of his anti-Vietnam War poem 'To Whom It May Concern'.

Not all the performers were so successful. Harry Fainlight, a British beat poet, attempted to read his poem 'The Spider', about a bad LSD trip, but his delivery was so mumbled that the audience grew restive and began to catcall. The Dutch poet Simon Vinkenoog attempted to encourage Fainlight and quieten the hecklers by jumping up on stage and shouting 'Love! Love! Love!' repeatedly while waving his arms about, but his intervention merely added to the confusion. In the end, Trocchi took Fainlight's mike from him with the words, 'Thank you, Harry, I think we've all heard enough of that now.' Meanwhile, Jeff Nuttall, later author of *Bomb Culture*, and the conceptual artist John Latham had painted themselves blue and dressed in overblown and very heavy costumes made out of books, which they planned to tear off one another during a staged happening. Unfortunately, compère Trocchi forgot to signal their entrance and they were kept waiting in the wings, in increasing discomfort, for far too long. Overcome by body paint and his weighty outfit, Latham eventually passed out. Whatever the individual successes and failures at the First International Poetry Incarnation, there can be no disputing its importance. According to Barry Miles, then working at Better Books in Charing Cross Road and one of its organisers, it marked 'the birth of the London underground' of the second half of the sixties. It was, in the words of Michael Horovitz, 'the moment when 8,000 people came together, looked round, and thought: this is a new beginning'.

Psychedelic Bohemia

That sense of generational solidarity and commitment to new ways of looking at life and society which had been felt by many of the participants in the First International Poetry Incarnation in 1965 was echoed in other events over the next two years. The launch of *International Times* (*IT*), which was to become the house magazine of the underground movement in the late sixties, took place in October 1966 at the Roundhouse, an old railway engine shed in Chalk Farm, and was advertised as a 'Pop/Op/Costume/Masque/Fantasy/Loon/Drag Ball'. Two thousand people turned up to hear Soft Machine and Pink Floyd take part in happenings and watch the films and light shows which were projected on to giant plastic sheets. According to Barry Miles, one of *IT*'s founders, who was present, 'People wore refraction lenses to indicate their third eye, they wore silver headdresses and long robes, spaceman outfits and rubber bondage wear... Paul McCartney, dressed in sheik's robes, strolled around with Jane Asher, Monica Vitti was with Michelangelo Antonioni, Alexander Trocchi tried to get in free by walking all the way up the railway tracks to the British Rail entrance; Mick Farren says someone saw a camel there but it seems unlikely.'

In less than a year *IT*, facing regular police harassment and the costs of several drugs cases in court, was in need of financial help. A benefit concert, known as the 14-Hour Technicolor Dream, was

INTERNATIONAL TIMES N°3, 1966

organised in the Great Hall of Alexandra Palace in north London. Music was provided by all the leading psychedelic bands of the era, from The Crazy World of Arthur Brown, with their leader sporting his trademark fiery helmet, to Soft Machine. Light shows and avant-garde films were projected on to giant white sheets hanging in the galleries at the sides of the main hall. Poets and guitar-strumming troubadours attempted to entertain the drifting crowds. Stalls offered candy floss, sweets and vegetarian food. Yoko Ono directed a piece of performance art, in which members of the audience were invited to use a pair of giant scissors to cut away parts of her clothing. Suzy Creamcheese, then girlfriend of organiser John 'Hoppy' Hopkins, sat outside a fibreglass igloo, handing out joints rolled from dried banana skins. Most of those who took them were already too high to judge whether or not these novelty spliffs had any great effect. In the centre of the hall was a fairground helter skelter, down which shrieking hippies slid. The event culminated in a performance by Pink Floyd as dawn broke and the first rays of the morning sun illuminated a vast rose window on the south-east front of the building. As 'Hoppy' Hopkins later recalled, 'The 14-Hour Technicolor Dream was a big event and a financial disaster. Most people were on drugs of one sort or another. It was a crest of a wave. It wasn't fully understood, but it was a landmark event.'

The previous year Hopkins had been one of the co-founders of another important, if short-lived, focal point of psychedelic bohemia. Together with the record producer Joe Boyd, he established the UFO Club in a former Irish dance hall in Tottenham Court Road. Bands that played there included the usual suspects (Pink Floyd, Soft Machine, The Crazy World of Arthur Brown) and light shows, avant-garde films by the likes of Kenneth Anger and Stan Brakhage, and improvisational dance troupes were all part of the entertainment. Opening from 10.30pm to 6am ('conveniently about the length of an acid trip', as Hopkins pointed out), the UFO soon became a magnet for the city's hippies and heads. Celebrities like Paul McCartney and The Who's Pete Townshend were regular visitors. Townshend was so impressed by Arthur Brown's theatrical performances, in which he came on stage with painted face mask and fiery headdress (on more than one occasion this had to be dowsed with pints of beer when the flames threatened to get out of control), that he persuaded his own record label to sign Brown. Brown's one big hit, inevitably called 'Fire', followed in 1968. Although later remembered rather dismissively by habitué John Peel as a place 'where all of us hippies

BEAUTIFUL
SOUND
LIGHT
TOUCH
STAREYE
BODYTASTE
EVERYONE IS
SAYING SO . . .

UFO

NOW — ALL NIGHT — TILL THE
FIRST TRAINS RUN ★ FEATURE MOVIE

FRIDAYS 10.30 p.m. 31 TOTTENHAM COURT ROAD

COMING COMING SOON FESTIVAL OF LOVE FEB. 10th

NEWSPAPER ADVERT FOR THE UFO CLUB

used to put on our kaftans and bells and beads and go and lie on the floor in an altered condition and listen to whatever was going on', there is no disputing the significance of the UFO Club.

Although it had closed by the end of 1967, after an unsuccessful move to the Roundhouse, it had provided a meeting place for like-minded individuals who created new artistic groupings. Exploding Galaxy, a commune and 'love-anarchist dance group' in Balls Pond Road, was the brainchild of two artists named Paul Keeler and David Medalla, and its early members were all people who had encountered one another at UFO. (Their first performance was at the 14-Hour Technicolor Dream.) Intent on challenging conventional notions of sexual identity, the Exploders all dressed out of a large chest filled with a variety of costumes and clothing. Whatever you fished out on a particular day determined both what you wore and who you were. If a man pulled out a skirt, he was a female for the day. During their lengthy, multimedia performances of dance and theatre, costumes of any kind often became an irrelevance, since they preferred to be nude. At the trial of three Exploders on drugs charges in 1968, the playwright and sometime MP Benn Levy gave a statement in their defence which reads like a description of bohemian life that could have been applied to Murger and his Parisian pals more than a century earlier. The Exploders, Levy said, 'are unacquisitive, as oblivious of elementary comfort as a classical religious order, unselfconsciously ascetic… they live in cheerful penury working away like beavers on projects that offer no prospect of serious remuneration… they dress and coif themselves egregiously, prompted not by fashion but by individual fancy.' Two out of the three Exploders were acquitted, but the Balls Pond commune soon came to an end.

Other communes formed, flourished briefly and dissolved all over London. There were also more trials, as the authorities turned upon the burgeoning counter-culture. The raid on Keith Richards' Sussex mansion, which resulted in charges being brought against Richards, Mick Jagger and the art dealer Robert Fraser, had been the most notorious drugs bust of the time, because of the fame of the individuals involved, but others followed. If these new psychedelic bohemians could not be charged with drugs offences, perhaps they could be targeted under obscenity laws. Barry Miles, one of the prime movers behind the First International Poetry Incarnation and the 14-Hour Technicolor Dream, was now running Indica Bookshop, which, with the financial assistance of Paul McCartney, had moved from its original premises in Mayfair to new ones in Southampton Row. The Indica not only became a mecca for those in search of offbeat and 'underground' literature, but the focus of a number of counter-cultural ventures, including Alex Trocchi's Project Sigma, a hugely ambitious attempt to create what its founder, in a manifesto, called 'an invisible insurrection of a million minds'. Project Sigma had swiftly come to grief during a weekend gathering in 1964, which had been disrupted by

Trocchi's chaotic drug-taking and heavy drinking, and was now reduced to little more than a name and a faint hope. Its office at Indica was hardly ever used. *International Times* (*IT*), launched the previous year at the Roundhouse, also took offices in the basement at Southampton Row. They were on the receiving end of several raids by the Obscene Publications Squad, since revealed as an epically corrupt unit of the Metropolitan Police during these years. In the worst of them, the police seized every piece of paper in the offices, including back issues, staff members' address books and even phone directories, in the hopes of finding obscene material lurking within them. After keeping them for three months without bringing any charges, they returned everything by the simple means of turning up at Southampton Row and hurling it all down the stairs to the basement.

The most famous of late sixties and early seventies assaults on freedom of speech remains the *OZ* trial of 1971. The magazine *OZ* had first appeared in Australia in 1963, but a British version was created soon after one of its original editors, Richard Neville, pitched up in London in 1966. The Obscene Publications Squad had its baleful eye on the underground press throughout the late sixties and the offices of *OZ*, like those of *IT*, were regularly raided during those years. However, the 'Schoolkids OZ' of May 1970 provided the authorities with the ideal opportunity to mount what was effectively a show trial. Neville and his fellow editors Jim Anderson and Felix Dennis had thrown the issue open to guest contributors who were schoolchildren (they included the future music journalist Charles Shaar Murray) and some of the results, particularly a sexualised parody of Rupert Bear in which the *Daily Express* cartoon character is equipped with a giant phallus, were deemed obscene. The editors were charged with 'intent... to debauch and corrupt the morals of young children and young persons within the realm and to arouse and implant in their minds lustful and perverted desires'. It was the start of one

INVITE TO ATTEND THE *OZ* TRIAL, 1971

of the longest and most surreal obscenity trials in British legal history. On one side were the three defendants and their roster of celebrity supporters, which included their lawyer, the playwright and barrister John Mortimer, George Melly, the comedian Marty Feldman and Edward de Bono, advocate of lateral thinking; on the other were the reactionary judge, Michael Argyle, and those who thought the permissiveness of the sixties had destroyed all that was best in society. Highlights of the trial and its aftermath included the Crown Prosecutor describing, at some length, his distaste for inflatable rubber dolls; the same prosecuting lawyer grilling a child psychologist on the sexual behaviour of young bears ('I'm very sorry, I'm not up to date on bears,' the psychologist replied); and the three defendants turning up to their appeal hearing dressed as schoolboys. In the end, Neville, Anderson and Dennis were found guilty of several of the offences with which they were charged and sentenced to varying periods of imprisonment. However, the judge's summing up and directions to the jury had been so blatantly biased that the sentences were overturned on appeal, although not before the three editors had had their long hair forcibly (and perhaps symbolically) shorn by the prison barber.

The Seventies and Punk

The OZ trial was one of many signs that the sixties were well and truly over and a new decade had begun. By the early seventies, the gentle ambience of psychedelic bohemia, in which stoned hippies contemplated the meaning of the universe to the accompaniment of Pink Floyd and Soft Machine, had long gone. A new and more confrontational avant-garde emerged. No one represented it better than the person who became known as Genesis P-Orridge. Born as Neil Andrew Megson, he grew up in Stockport and Solihull. After dropping out of a university course in Hull, he arrived in London in 1968 and spent time in the Exploding Galaxy commune before tiring of the city and heading north again. Back in Hull, Megson officially adopted the name of Genesis P-Orridge and joined forces with Christine Newby (aka Cosey Fanni Tutti) to create a group called COUM Transmissions. Returning to London in 1973 and taking up residence in a damp basement studio in Hackney, Genesis and Cosey embarked on a journey to the outer limits of performance art. In the words of Barry Miles, 'COUM appeared naked, they slashed their bodies with knives, they sloshed around in stage blood and real blood, they performed and simulated sex, they drank urine and vomited.' Cosey took work as a porn model to further her explorations of female sexuality and a week-long series of COUM events at the ICA in 1976, which included some of the results of her ongoing research, aroused the spluttering wrath of Tory MP Nicholas Fairbairn. He told the *Daily Mail* that the show was 'a sickening outrage. Obscene. Evil. Public money is being wasted here to destroy the morality of our society'. Briefly, the COUM show

WORKING-CLASS BOHEMIA

October 19th-26th 1976

SEXUAL TRANSGRESSIONS NO. 5

PROSTITUTION

COUM Transmissions:- Founded 1969. Members (active) Oct 76 - P. Christopherson,
                    Cosey Fanni Tutti,Genesis P-Orridge.Studio in London.Had a
kind of manifesto in July/August Studio International 1976. Performed their works
in Palais des Beaux Arts,Brussels; Musee d'Art Moderne, Paris; Galleria Borgogna,
Milan; A.I.R. Gallery, London; and took part in Arte Inglese Oggi, Milan survey of
British Art in 1976. November/December 1976 they perform in Los Angeles Institute
of Contemporary Art;Deson Gallery,Chicago;N.A.M.E. Gallery,Chicago and in Canada.
This exhibition was prompted as a comment on survival in Britain,and themselves.

2 years have passed since the above photo of Cosey in a magazine inspired this
exhibition.Cosey has appeared in 40 magazines now as a deliberate policy.All of
these framed form the core of this exhibition.Different ways of seeing and using
Cosey with her consent,produced by people unaware of her reasons,as a woman and an
artist, for participating.In that sense,pure views.In line with this all the photo
documentation shown was taken,unbidden by COUM by people who decided on their own
to photograph our actions.How other people saw and recorded us as information.Then
there are xeroxes of our press cuttings,media write ups.COUM as raw material.All of
them,who are they about and for? The only things here made by COUM are our objects.
Things used in actions,intimate (previously private) assemblages made just for us.
Everything in the show is or sale at a price,even the people. For us the party
on the opening night is the key to our stance,the most important performance.We
shall also do a few actions as counterpoint later in the week.

    PERFORMANCES: Wed 20th 1pm - Fri 22nd 7pm

                   Sat 23rd 1pm - Sun 24th 7pm

INSTITUTE OF CONTEMPORARY ARTS LIMITED
NASH HOUSE THE MALL LONDON S.W.I.   BOX OFFICE Telephone 01-930-6393

POSTER FOR A COUM EVENT AT THE ICA, 1976

at the ICA became a *cause célèbre*. Throbbing Gristle, the band which Genesis and Cosey formed, pushed back further boundaries with their dodgy fascination with bondage, pornography and Nazi iconography and with performances that were more outrageous than anything the punk bands that sprang into being at much the same time would ever offer. It's probably just as well that Nicholas Fairbairn is not known to have attended one of their gigs.

COUM Transmissions and Throbbing Gristle provided one of the most extreme examples of a growing recognition in the seventies that sexuality was not a given, but an area for debate. Throughout the sixties, although sexual attitudes, in many ways, had undergone a revolution, in other ways they had remained stubbornly the same. For many of the bohemians of Swinging London, men were still men, women were handmaidens or groupies, and homosexuality was an only recently legalised aberration. In the following decade there was a growing recognition in more avant-garde circles that sexual identities could be fluid rather than fixed. One of the more genial figures at the forefront of changing attitudes to (and depictions of) sexuality in the arts was Derek Jarman. Born in Middlesex in 1942, Jarman studied at the Slade School of Art and then worked as a stage and film designer, getting his big break with the Ken Russell film *The Devils* in 1970. He moved on to directing his own movies, beginning with *Sebastiane* in 1976, a retelling of the story of St Sebastian's martyrdom. Notable for its homoeroticism and male nudity, it may well be the only film with dialogue mostly in Latin (with English subtitles) ever to get a general cinema release. Jarman went on to make some of the most distinctive British movies of the next decade, including *Jubilee*, arguably the only successful 'punk' film, *The Tempest*, a startlingly original version of the Shakespeare play, and *Caravaggio*, a characteristically idiosyncratic biopic of the Italian artist.

He was also one of the leading lights in the Alternative Miss World competitions, which took place intermittently throughout the seventies. The first was held in artist Andrew Logan's studio in an old jigsaw puzzle factory in Hackney. The traditional Miss World organisation sued this gay alternative, but, defended in court by a young barrister named Tony Blair, Logan and his friends won the case and the show continued. Jarman himself won the third Alternative Miss World, held at Logan's new studio in Butler's Wharf in 1975, as Miss Crêpe Suzette. His costumes consisted of 'a Jeanne d'Arc suit of armour with a built-in sound system' and a silver diamanté dress accessorised with snorkelling flippers and 'a headdress made from a green rubber frog'. Outfits grew ever more flamboyant as the Alternative Miss World became more popular. The 1978 event, held in a blue circus tent on Clapham Common, was won by Miss Carriage, but many thought that the prize should have gone to Miss Consumer Products, the art dealer James Birch, who appeared for his beachwear costume as a tube of Ambre Solaire, squirting white gobbets of liquid in the direction of the audience. Logan's Alternative Miss World has continued to the present day and is now a much-loved event in the London calendar.

By the mid-seventies, as the Alternative Miss World flourished, punk was also beginning to stir. In the King's Road boutique, Sex, run by Malcolm McLaren and Vivienne Westwood, a new look was being created and the Sex Pistols were set on the road to national notoriety. One of punk's first gathering places was in the unlikely setting of Louise's, a lesbian club in Poland Street, Soho. Run by a stylish Frenchwoman, it catered mainly for middle-aged, middle-class lesbians, but, when it was discovered by teenage proto-punks like Siouxsie Sioux and others from the so-called Bromley Contingent, Louise was happy to open her doors to a new clientele. McLaren, Westwood and assorted Sex Pistols were soon regulars and, as punk got under way, its enthusiasts began to outnumber Louise's original customers. The club closed, but the punks soon had other places to go. The 100 Club was still thriving and, in September 1976, was the venue for a two-

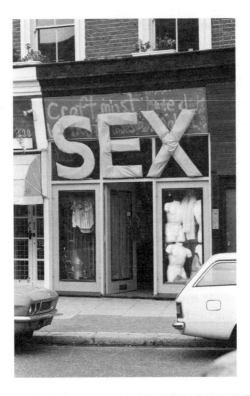

MALCOLM MCLAREN AND VIVIENNE WESTWOOD SEX BOUTIQUE
IN KING'S ROAD, 1976

day punk festival which featured the Sex Pistols, the Clash and Siouxsie and the Banshees. This was the latter's first appearance on stage and they were hampered by the fact that few of them could play an instrument and none of them knew any songs. In the end, their act turned out to be an improvisational one, with Siouxsie reciting The Lord's Prayer and any other stray bits of text she could dredge up from her memory, while Sid Vicious banged relentlessly on a drum kit in the background. One of those watching the Sex Pistols was John Walters, then the producer of John Peel's radio show, who was wondering whether or not this already controversial band was worth booking for a session. He decided against doing so, largely because Johnny Rotten reminded him of teenage thugs he had taught when he was an art teacher. 'I thought, "There's a boy I wouldn't ask to give out the scissors",' he later recalled. Punk had swiftly gained a reputation for violence at gigs. It was often justified. Sid Vicious had already attacked music journalist Nick Kent at an earlier Sex Pistols show at the 100 Club and, on the second day of the festival, was arrested for throwing a beer glass which shattered and blinded a girl in one eye.

The 100 Club festival was a catalyst for the burgeoning punk scene. Many of those in the audience, including Gaye Advert, Shane McGowan, Viv Albertine and Chrissie Hynde, went on to create their own bands. The Roxy Club, which became *the* club for the punks, opened in Neal Street, Covent Garden in late 1976. (Generation X played a pre-Christmas gig there, although the official opening was by The Clash on New Year's Day, 1977.) A dark basement with a low ceiling which rapidly became the target for the heads of pogoing fans, the Roxy was the venue for punk excess throughout the first four months of 1977. As a hit list of bands from The Damned and The Buzzcocks to X-Ray Spex and The Slits played, their devotees made merry by running riot. Glasses were smashed, graffiti sprayed across the walls, phlegm flew and beer, blood and vomit carpeted the dance floor. The bands themselves were often as chaotically unruly as their fans and, for a brief few months, a new, anarchic bohemia seemed to have arrived. The dawn eventually proved a false one and, within a year, punk had either collapsed in on itself or was well on the way to crass commercialisation, but it was a heady period for its true adherents.

Epilogue

BOHEMIA TODAY

*'I don't know where you go to find bohemia now.
I asked one of my young friends and she looked at me
and she asked me seriously: "Have you tried online?"'*
IRMA KURTZ, 2015

SOME WOULD ARGUE that the punks were London's last true bohemians. In the 40 years since punk's heyday there have been no movements in which genuine outsiders to society and culture have asserted their identities. Is this true? Or has bohemia continued to thrive during those decades? If so, where should we look for London bohemians in the eighties, nineties and beyond? Perhaps it should be amongst the performance artists who proliferated in those decades. The Neo-Naturists were a group, fresh from a variety of art schools and squatting in a house in Fitzrovia, which included the Binnie sisters, Christine and Jennifer, and Jennifer's then boyfriend, the now-famous cross-dressing potter Grayson Perry. Their urge to strip off their clothes, daub themselves with body paint and become living works of art spiced up many an otherwise dull day in early eighties London. Their most ambitious event, involving 15 people living in the nude and undertaking themed performances for a week, took place at

EPILOGUE: BOHEMIA TODAY

a gallery in Wapping. One day was Macbeth Day, on which they performed a truncated, ten-minute version of the Shakespeare play. Seven witches took to the stage, rather than the traditional three, because so many people wanted to play them, and Grayson Perry, covered in a mixture of porridge oats and body paint to simulate the texture of tree bark, and holding above his head large bunches of buddleia, represented Birnam Wood. Unfortunately, the porridge set hard, making it extremely painful for him to move, and Birnam Wood had extreme difficulty in coming to high Dunsinane Hill. It took him hours to wash the mixture off.

More extreme and transgressive were the Australian Leigh Bowery and the dandyish English artist Sebastian Horsley. Born in Melbourne in 1961, Bowery arrived in London in 1980 and was soon an unforgettable figure on the club scene. Part performance artist, part entrepreneur (his club Taboo was a great success) and part fashion designer, he was unique. 'I try to have as much sex, violence and gore as possible in the shows,' he once remarked of his performances as a living artwork, '– pee drinking, vomiting, enemas and fake blood. It's a formula which always seems to please.' In Bowery's most characteristic performance, repeated many times, he appeared on stage in a kind of gigantic fat suit, adding to his own enormous girth. Within it, naked and strapped upside down to his stomach, was his long-term collaborator Nicola Bateman. Screaming and yelling, Bowery would lie back and 'give birth' to Bateman as she emerged from between his legs, smeared in blood and petroleum jelly and trailing strings of sausages as an umbilical cord behind her. As Boy George, a regular witness to the performance, once noted, this 'never ceased to impress or revolt'. In the years before his death in 1994, Bowery also became one of Lucian Freud's favourite models, his vast bulk rendered in graphic detail on the painter's canvases.

Sebastian Horsley was a Yorkshire-born artist who took up residence in Soho's Meard Street and soon became as famous for his extreme lifestyle as for his work. Addicted to a small pharmacy of drugs, Horsley was also an enthusiastic and unrepentant user of prostitutes, although his own home had a sign attached to it that read: 'This Is Not a Brothel. There Are No Prostitutes at This Address'. In 2000, in preparation for a series of paintings on the subject of the crucifixion, he travelled to the Philippines to take part in a religious ritual in which participants attempted to reproduce Christ's agony on the cross. Horsley was himself nailed by his hands and his feet to a cross and, when the footrest broke, he passed out and came close to suffering life-threatening injuries.

Perhaps 1980s bohemians were to be found in the clubs where new music and new fashions were created. The Blitz in Great Queen Street, Covent Garden was Steve Strange's club, where the peacocks of what was to become the New Romantic subculture, including Boy George, Rusty Egan and Strange himself, paraded in their finery. Later in the eighties, Leigh Bowery's Taboo, held in the Circus Maximus disco in Leicester Square, became the place to see and be seen. The door policy was encapsulated by Bowery himself, when he remarked that would-be clubbers at Taboo should, 'Dress as though your life depends on it or don't bother.' Bowery himself always followed his own precept – nobody who saw him, for instance, in puffball face mask, sequined boots and push-up bra, but otherwise butt naked, was ever likely to forget the experience – though others flirted similarly with the outrageous.

In the late eighties and nineties, it was a very different kind of club where the spirit of bohemianism was alleged to be best preserved. The Groucho Club in Dean Street was founded in 1985 (taking its name from Groucho Marx, who once sent a telegram to the Friar's Club in Beverly Hills which read: 'Please accept my resignation. I don't want to belong to any club that will accept people like me as a member.') and soon gained a certain notoriety. Certainly many members of the Groucho wanted the wider public to believe that it was upholding bohemian traditions. There was a kind of self-

STEVE STRANGE AND JULIA AT THE BLITZ CLUB IN COVENT GARDEN. 1980

consciousness in their bad behaviour. Paradoxically, this had the effect of making them seem less free and unconventional than their predecessors. Old-style bohemians behaved as they did because it came naturally to them; Groucho bohemians always seemed to have one eye on the photographers and the gossip columnists. Stories of dissipation flourished, passed on and doubtless embellished by the participants and fellow members. Perhaps the best-known remains the one about a coke- and drink-fuelled lock-in involving Damien Hirst, the actor Keith Allen and Blur bassist Alex James, who all hid under the pool table to avoid detection when the club closed. After a night of substance consumption, they took over service for breakfast the following morning when the Groucho reopened, all minus their trousers because, they claimed, it was 'no trousers day'. When Stephen Fry arrived and ordered sausages, a half-naked Hirst walked out from behind the bar with his cock on a plate and presented it to the TV polymath. 'I said a sausage, not a chipolata,' Fry is reputed to have replied.

Where does all this leave bohemia today? Is it a thing of the past? Nostalgia for an authentic bohemia that once existed, but has now disappeared, has long been expressed. 'Whatever else bohemia may be it is almost always yesterday,' the American critic Arthur Bartlett Maurice wrote in 1916 and the belief that true bohemia has been destroyed either by the influx of amateur, part-time bohemians, or by changes in society that have rendered commonplace what was once outrageous is a recurring one throughout the twentieth century. Thirty years later, Stanley Jackson, author of *An Indiscreet Guide to Soho*, was already claiming that, 'If you are in search of the bohemianism of the novels, Soho will disappoint you today.' Perhaps the reality is that we are all bohemians now. Ordinary Londoners today speak, dress and behave in ways that, a few generations in the past, would have been categorised as irredeemably bohemian. And when everybody is a bohemian, then nobody is.

Bibliography

Bohemian London is aimed at a general readership, not a scholarly one. For that reason, I have chosen not to weigh down the text with footnotes and academic annotations. However, this is a list of the books I have found most useful while writing the book and from which I have drawn most of the material.

Adams, Jad, *Hideous Absinthe: A History of the Devil in a Bottle*, IB Tauris, 2004

Adams, Jad, *Madder Music, Stronger Wine: The Life of Ernest Dowson, Poet and Decadent*, Tauris Parke, 2000

Angier, Carole, *Jean Rhys*, Andre Deutsch, 1990

Anon (ed), *Mr Punch in Bohemia*, The Educational Book Company, 1910

Arnold, Catharine, *City of Sin: London and Its Vices*, Simon & Schuster, 2010

Barrow, Andrew, *Quentin & Philip: A Double Portrait*, Macmillan, 2002

Bristow, Roger, *The Last Bohemians: The Two Roberts – Colquhoun and MacBryde*, Sansom & Co, 2009

Brooker, Peter, *Bohemia in London: The Social Scene of Early Modernism*, Palgrave Macmillan, 2004

Burgess, Anthony, *Little Wilson and Big God*, Heinemann, 1987

Christie, William, *Dylan Thomas: A Literary Life*, Palgrave Macmillan, 2014

Connolly, Cressida, *The Rare and the Beautiful: The Lives of the Garmans*, Fourth Estate, 2004

Cook, Matt, *London and the Culture of Homosexuality 1885–1914*, Cambridge University Press, 2003

Cronin, Anthony, *Dead as Doornails*, Calder & Boyars, 1976

Cross, Nigel, *The Common Writer: Life in Nineteenth Century Grub Street*, Cambridge University Press, 1985

David, Hugh, *The Fitzrovians*, Michael Joseph, 1988

Deghy, Guy and Waterhouse, Keith, *The Café Royal: Ninety Years of Bohemia*, Hutchinson, 1955

Donaldson, Willie, *Brewer's Rogues, Villains and Eccentrics*, Cassell, 2002

Farson, Dan, *The Gilded Gutter Life of Francis Bacon*, Century, 1994

Farson, Dan, *Soho in the Fifties*, Michael Joseph, 1987

Fiber, Sally, *The Fitzroy: An Autobiography of a London Tavern*, Temple House, 1995

Ford, Ford Madox (Ed. Max Hutchings), *Return to Yesterday*, Carcanet, 1999

Fraser, Robert, *The Chameleon Poet: A Life of George Barker*, Jonathan Cape, 2001

Gatrell, Vic, *The First Bohemians*, Allen Lane, 2013

Glinert, Ed, *West End Chronicles*, Allen Lane, 2007

Gordon, Lois, *Nancy Cunard: Heiress, Muse, Political Idealist*, Columbia University Press, 2007

Graña, César and Graña, Marigay, *On Bohemia*, Transaction Publishers, 1990

Hamnett, Nina, *Laughing Torso*, Constable, 1932

Haslam, Dave, *Life After Dark: A History of British Nightclubs and Music Venues*, Simon & Schuster, 2015

Hewison, Robert, *In Anger*, Weidenfeld & Nicolson, 1981

Hewison, Robert, *Under Siege*, Weidenfeld & Nicolson, 1977

Hoare, Philip, *Oscar Wilde's Last Stand*, Duckworth, 1997

Holroyd, Michael, *Augustus John: The New Biography*, Chatto & Windus, 1996

Houlbrook, Matt, *Queer London: Perils and Pleasures in the Sexual Metropolis 1918–57*, University of Chicago Press, 2005

Jackson, Holbrook, *The Eighteen Nineties*, Grant Richards, 1913

Jackson, Stanley, *An Indiscreet Guide to Soho*, Muse Arts Ltd, 1946

Kaczynski, Richard, *Perdurabo: The Life of Aleister Crowley*, North Atlantic Books, 2010

King, Viva, *The Weeping and the Laughter*, Macdonald & Jane's, 1976

Kohn, Marek, *Dope Girls: The Birth of the British Drug Underground*, Lawrence & Wishart, 1992

Luke, Michael, *David Tennant and the Gargoyle Years*, Weidenfeld & Nicolson, 1991

Lycett, Andrew, *Dylan Thomas: A New Life*, Orion, 2003

BIBLIOGRAPHY

MacInnes, Colin, *England, Half English*, MacGibbon & Kee, 1961

Maclaren-Ross, Julian, *Memoirs of the Forties*, Alan Ross, 1965

May, Betty, *Tiger Woman*, Duckworth, 2014

Medley, Robert, *Drawn from the Life*, Faber, 1983

Melly, George, *Owning Up: The Trilogy*, Penguin, 2000

Miles, Barry, *London Calling: A Countercultural History of London Since 1945*, Atlantic, 2010

Moraes, Henrietta, *Henrietta*, Hamish Hamilton, 1994

Morton, James, *Gangland Soho*, Piatkus, 2008

Muddiman, Bernard, *The Men of the Nineties*, Henry Danielson, 1920

Nelson, James G, *Publisher to the Decadents: Leonard Smithers in the Careers of Beardsley, Wilde, Dowson*, Pennsylvania State University Press, 2000

Nevinson, CRW, *Paint and Prejudice*, Methuen, 1937

Nicholson, Virginia, *Among the Bohemians*, Viking, 2002

Pentelow, Mike and Rowe, Marsha, *Characters of Fitzrovia*, Chatto & Windus, 2001

Peppiatt, Michael, *Francis Bacon: Anatomy of an Enigma*, Weidenfeld & Nicolson, 1996

Ransome, Arthur, *Bohemia in London*, Chapman & Hall, 1907

Rogers, Pat, *Grub Street: Studies in a Subculture*, Methuen, 1972

Sinclair, Andrew, *War Like a Wasp: The Lost Decade of the Forties*, Hamish Hamilton, 1989

Sloan, John, *John Davidson, First of the Moderns: A Literary Biography*, Oxford University Press, 1995

Sturgis, Matthew, *Passionate Attitudes: The English Decadence of the 1890s*, Macmillan, 1995

Summers, Judith, *Soho: A History of London's Most Colourful Neighbourhood*, Bloomsbury, 1989

Sutin, Lawrence, *Do What Thou Wilt: A Life of Aleister Crowley*, St Martin's Press, 2000

Sweet, Matthew, *Inventing the Victorians*, Faber, 2001

Tames, Richard, *Soho Past*, Historical Publications, 1994

Taylor, DJ, *Bright Young People: The Rise and Fall of a Generation 1918–1940*, Chatto & Windus, 2007

Walkowitz, Judith R, *Nights Out: Life in Cosmopolitan London*, Yale University Press, 2012

Weintraub, Stanley, *Beardsley*, WH Allen, 1967

Willetts, Paul, *Fear and Loathing in Fitzrovia: The Bizarre Life of Julian Maclaren-Ross*, Dewi Lewis, 2003

White, Jerry, *London in the Nineteenth Century*, Jonathan Cape, 2007

White, Jerry, *London in the Twentieth Century*, Viking, 2001

Wilson, Elizabeth, *The Bohemians*, IB Tauris, 2000

Wyndham, Joan, *Love Is Blue*, Heinemann, 1986

Wyndham, Joan, *Love Lessons*, Heinemann, 1986

Yorke, Malcolm, *The Spirit of Place: Nine Neo-Romantic Artists and Their Times*, Constable, 1988

Fiction

Camberton, Roland (with an introduction by Iain Sinclair), *Scamp*, New London Editions, 2010

Gissing, George, *New Grub Street*, Penguin Classics, 1968 (first published in 1891)

MacInnes, Colin, *Absolute Beginners*, MacGibbon & Kee, 1959

Taylor, Terry, *Baron's Court, All Change*, New London Editions, 2011 (first published by MacGibbon & Kee, 1961)

Thackeray, William Makepeace, *Pendennis*, Oxford University Press (World's Classics), 1999 (first published by Bradbury & Evans, 1848–50)

Waterhouse, Keith, *Soho*, Sceptre, 2001

Waugh, Evelyn, *Vile Bodies*, Chapman & Hall, 1930

Wilson, Colin, *Adrift in Soho*, New London Editions, 2011 (first published by Gollancz in 1961)

Index

INDEX

INDEX